The
BALANCE
POINT

MASTER THE
WORK-LIFE BALANCE,
LOVE WHAT YOU DO, AND BECOME AN
UNSTOPPABLE ENTREPRENEUR

JORDAN RING

Publishing services provided by 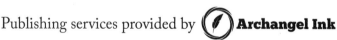 **Archangel Ink**

ISBN-13: 978-1-942761-96-9

FOREWORD

Several months ago, Jordan and I had a conversation about managing social/recreational time with productive time, which led us to chat about generating wealth vs. enjoying its fruits. If you're a current or aspiring entrepreneur you may have asked these questions too. How do I find time and energy for my 5-9 passion project/side hustle when I still need my 9-5 to pay the bills? What tradeoffs am I willing to make?

At one point, I made barely four figures a month but was fortunate enough to work digitally. The time others would spend working or commuting, I was able to redirect toward cooking big batches of rice and beans for pennies on the dollar. I substituted walking and bicycling for a car payment or even a subway pass. It was an elegant solution: more free time meant I could create wealth in-house rather than outsourcing necessities.

Having free time had other benefits as well. If I traveled, I could take trips mid-week or at off hours to find the best deals. Long leisurely lunch specials were on the menu if I wanted to dine out, since I wasn't rushing back to the office.

And of course I had space to discover my patterns and organize my days around my most productive periods. Working late into the night or early mornings when distractions were scarce was no trouble, nor was taking off several days when I needed a breather. If I needed to attend to errands during business hours, I didn't have to scramble or cash out paid time off.

On the other hand, stability can be hard to come by on your own. For the first several years or more as an entrepreneur, income may be unsteady. You may need to forego the newest phone, the nicest car, the swankiest restaurants, or maybe even your gym membership if you're all in on your venture.

It can also be lonely and isolating. As unpleasant as office politics can be, there's something satisfying about going into a shared physical space with co-workers and moving toward a common purpose. Having regular interaction focused on an outside goal provides an organic pretext and space for relationships to develop. The work-from-home life doesn't inherently offer the same.

And neither does it offer a clear separation of work from home, nor labor from leisure. Without systems in place or a strong sense of focus, you can become distracted and end the day in a rut after spinning your wheels chasing one diversion after the next, with boxes on your to-do list left unchecked. "Time off" can bleed into your productive life, and work easily slips into your down time.

Again: trade offs.

What do you value, what do you need, and what can you live without?

In this book, Jordan approaches these questions in the context of balance. What is it to live a balanced life? What are your emotional, spiritual and philosophical underpinnings to that question? And notably, as is Jordan's specialty, what are some practical steps you can take to finding ways forward?

I've had the good fortune to know the author for several years. I've seen him take the leap of faith from working at an independent living facility care-taking for those in need, to full-time author, coach and digital nomad. One quality I've long appreciated and admired is his willingness to learn, to take his knocks, and make the best of his situation even when things go awry. And it is this willingness to continually experiment, adapt, and ponder that has rewarded him with new opportunities.

It is also what qualifies him to speak on the matter at hand. He's forthright in his strengths and shortcomings, and has the requisite willingness to self-reflect, and reverse engineer his progress. He's also sharp enough and empathic enough to make it relatable and useful.

So read through these chapters and experiment with his eleven axes to see if you can't also find a bit more balance in your life.

—Rob Archangel

Owner, Archangel Ink

CONTENTS

INTRODUCTION

BALANCE: THE KEY TO UNLOCKING SUSTAINABLE GROWTH, SUCCESS, AND LONG-TERM HAPPINESS

"Balance is a feeling derived from being whole and complete; it's a sense of harmony. It is essential to maintaining quality in life and work."
—Joshua Osenga

I don't have great balance. I've literally fallen standing up on more than one occasion. It's probably an issue with my inner ear. I've swayed to one side or the other since I was a kid.

It's no wonder my entrepreneurial endeavors over the past few years have been mired with a back-and-forth motion strong enough to make the doggiest of seadogs queasy. I wasn't able to pick a direction and stick with it, and my entrepreneurial growth stymied, often painfully. I found my hands in too many cookie jars at once, with my forward progress minimal in just about all of them.

More recently though, the pendulum is reaching more of a middle point. I'm finding that I have more time to do the things I really want to do, have fun in life, and enjoy the work too. This balance point is helping me find major success in business and in my personal life as I grow and achieve more than I ever dreamed possible.

I want to help you find the same balance point, as it holds the secret to long-term success and well being. Finding your balance point starts with answering one question.

I'm not ashamed to admit that I recently watched *The Notebook*, and ended up loving it. At one point, Ryan Gosling's character yelled at his counterpart and love interest Rachel McAdams, "What is it you want!?"

This is a question most of us have either struggled with or continue to struggle with. What is it we really want out of this one life? What do we want to do with our time? Is what I am doing bringing about any meaning to me, or to anyone else for that matter?

Life is meant to be lived with passion. It's what we are meant to do. Life isn't a dull, meaningless, and never-ending struggle. Life is a beautiful adventure we are blessed to have!

But too much passion can often lead us astray. If we err on the side of too much passion and don't find the appropriate opposing balance of purpose, we might end up whittling the days away on wood carvings no one is buying.

As entrepreneurs, we are more susceptible to this than most. We are in charge of our daily agenda and activities. We run the show (and wouldn't have it any other way), but we often end up spending late nights on email, stuck at a coworking space on a Sunday (isn't this just a cool way to say "working at the office?"), or tallying 100 hours in any given week to finish up everything we said yes to.

To find the perfect middle ground between making money and having fun, we must seek balance in all areas of life. If we master the art of saying no to good ideas to free up time for great ones, if we know when it's okay to multitask or give our full attention, and if we know when enough is enough and we finally shut down our laptop, we would find happiness and contentment right around the corner.

Life as an entrepreneur is fulfilling, but if we aren't careful it can also be exhausting and detrimental to our long-term health. If we burn out early our potential is squandered. Striking a work/life balance is not only a want, it's a need. If we can't find a way to enjoy the life we are crafting for ourselves, then why are we doing what we're doing? What's the point of bucking the system if we just toss ourselves into something worse? I don't know about you, but I don't want to work eighty hours per week with nothing to look forward to around the corner. I want to know I am building something that will last in order to continue to help others and produce passive income as I move on to other endeavors.

But what's the answer to this balance dilema?

It's easy to know that drinking a cup of green tea is a better decision than eating a donut, but when it comes to taking action versus planning, taking a trip or pulling a week of all nighters to finish a major project, or spending time with family versus closing out a major deal at your firm, balance issues arrive. When two really good things come at odds, we must make a choice and consider the consequences.

In order to become an unstoppable entrepreneur we must learn to strike the balance point between two good opposing forces and not get stuck on either side.

If we:

- Spend too much time on our business it might take off, but we might lose precious time with our children.

- Continue to take calculated but high-stakes risks we might get lucky, but it also might cost us everything.

- Read everything we can get our hands on, but never do anything with the content we consumed, no one wins.

Just because something is out of sync and wrong doesn't mean we throw caution to the wind and expend whatever energy necessary to right the ship. We need to be careful to look at all angles and carefully and thoughtfully adjust as needed. Too much of a good thing can very well be a bad thing. Too much entrepreneuring and we are lost in Boston without a GPS.

The more I experience life on this Earth, the more I realize balance is the key to it all. Whether I am running around like a headless chicken trying to finish work tasks, or moving slowly on a Saturday morning, I am convinced of the power of balance.

But balance is elusive. Even when you think you've gotten the hang of it, life throws a curveball at you and you are forced to switch things up. As such, mastery is highly difficult. Even more difficult is the fact that every area of your life has an intimate need for balance, yet there is no one-size-fits-all cure. So what do you do?

This book will give you a glimpse into what it looks like to live a balanced life. I'm not perfect and would never claim to be, but I've discovered secrets on how to hustle like crazy, fulfill my purpose, and still have fun doing it. This isn't due to any magical formula, but a consistent approach to health, wellness, and achieving a sense of balance through intentional living.

I get to spend every day with the woman of my dreams. Due to the hard work we've endured over the past few years, we now get to both claim "digital nomad" status, travel wherever and whenever we want, and consistently work together at a high level. Becoming balanced and well-rounded people led us to this point, and I will discuss how you can achieve your goals as well.

I'll be asking you a lot of questions throughout the book. Use them as a guide to continue doing what you are doing well, and to make a change in your life if needed. I'm convinced no one can truly change unless they decide to for themselves. Balance can't be found if you aren't ready to change.

The way forward is different for each individual. Maybe you are excellent at taking action, but suck at planning. You will need to err on the side of the coin you generally don't follow. This is not so much to flip-flop to the other side as it is to experience it and see what you may be missing.

Asking questions is the catalyst for growth. Don't worry if you don't know how to answer right away. You picked up this book for a reason. Question, ponder, act, experience, and grow.

Your mission in the following chapters is to identify the side you tend to fall on most within the primary struggle areas of work-life balance. When you identify your weak area, vow to err on the other side for a while. If you are usually tentative when it comes to taking action and enjoy the planning stages, stop thinking and start doing. If you tend to stay at home and avoid crowds, go against your modus operandi and spend time with people.

Growth and balance occur when we get outside of our normal routine. It allows us to see that the other side isn't all bad, and instead can be used to become a better version of ourselves.

We will be tackling the following eleven balance-point struggle areas for entrepreneurs:

1) Preparation vs. Action

2) Work vs. Play

3) Yes vs. No

4) Purpose vs. Passion

5) Reactive vs. Proactive

6) Intention vs. Perception

7) Consumption vs. Production

8) Instant Win vs. Delayed Gratification

9) Hustle vs. Health

10) 80 vs. 20

11) Potential vs. Contentment

In short sections at the beginning of each chapter we will look through the eyes of a fictional character named Andrew. We'll see how mastering these eleven struggle points will bring success, love, and abundant joy into your life.

Then, each chapter will provide tips, strategies, and resources to reach the balance point between the axes. And finally, you'll take note of where you fall on the spectrum to build your own personal balance blueprint.

Let's jump in and get some balance going.

- -

Before you dive in, I have a free bonus to offer you.

In addition to the information already provided in this book, I've created a helpful resource to help you identify your personal balance-point struggles.

To access your free bonus content, visit JMRing.com/BalanceBook Bonus

You'll get out of this book what you put in. Are you ready to find balance?

CHAPTER ONE

PREPARATION VS. ACTION

"An idea not coupled with action will never get any bigger than the brain cell it occupied."
—Arnold H. Glasow

"Failing to plan is planning to fail"
—Alan Lakein

Andrew took one last look at the building on 401 Glass Street Northwest and turned around. He was done. He had just quit and would never look back. He was on his own now. As he strode determinedly down the street he tossed his stack of glossy business cards in the trash and made his way home.

He hadn't come to this decision lightly. The weeks and weeks of tedious budget meetings with Chloe, his wife of over five years, almost made him want to stay at his current job. The way she said "Well now, honey..." was almost more than he could bear when he told her about his plan to leave. But in the end, she had agreed with his decision to move forward with his plans, to "give his dream a chance," as she put it.

What struck him as odd in that moment as he walked away was how calm he felt. He had just given up on a steady job with health insurance, a walk-in freezer with cold drinks in the break room, and an on-staff masseuse. Thinking about the daily neck rubs almost made him turn back, but no! He had made up his mind. Those perks weren't worth the indentured servitude that came along with them.

Andrew smiled as he thought about his boss's face when he handed in his two weeks. Confusion mixed with what? A hint of jealousy maybe? He scoffed at the thought. No need to feel sorry for Damien, he only had two years left until he retired and was also free of the corporate shackles.

As he walked the path he had trod for the last five years, Andrew's lips curled into a goofy smile. Everybody started looking at him as he made his way down the street. He was now a full-time entrepreneur who did everything on his schedule and his dime, and he didn't care how he looked in that moment.

He was the boss. He was in charge. He could sleep till 10 AM and wear his boxers around the house. He could sip martinis by his pool (when he could afford a pool) on a Tuesday afternoon.

He would be living the life, with a little bit of work thrown in here and there.

Now that Andrew was free, he could focus on the idea that had kept him up at night for months. The idea his wife had called crazy, an idea she was sure would bankrupt them. But it was an idea that he knew could change their lives—if he could just find the financial backing for it.

Up until this point he had lived his entire life with far too much planning and very little action. He couldn't wait to test out his action muscle and get his hands dirty trying out some of his best ideas.

- -

Action is the lifeblood of any good plan, but any good action step is rooted in strategy and starts with a great idea.

There's no magic formula for the exact amount of time you should spend strategizing, nor is there a concrete breakdown of when you should execute plans. But you probably know which one you find more comfortable spending time in, and which one you struggle with. The best strategy is to err on the side of what you struggle with the most. If you leap before you look, take a step back and plan. If you consistently face analysis paralysis, condition yourself to take a big chance and go for the action every once in a while.

I'll come clean here. I'm a huge fan of taking action steps instead of planning. I think action beats planning 90% of the time. "Just figure it out as you go" is often the catalyst for actually figuring things out.

But the initial setup to any small business is key. As entrepreneurs, we know things will blow up if no planning gets done. A good plan based on solid ideas is essential to achieving long-term success.

This is the balance point of action and preparation.

The key for successful entrepreneurs is to find the perfect sweet spot between the two. We must find a way to plan well and also strike forth and take action on the plan. It starts with coming up with our actionable ideas, and then being okay giving up on all others to pursue our unique path.

What to do with Great Ideas (and How to Dump Bad Ideas)

Successful people have a particular skill dialed up and ready to go: They are able to take ideas from the void and, using a method I call "idea cultivation," they turn good ideas into reality, shelve other ideas for later use, and pitch the bad ideas.

In this section we are going to talk about how to cultivate the best ideas out of all your ideas. When I refer to ideas in this chapter I use the term interchangeably with goals and tasks.

There are three types of ideas:

1) Ideas you can take action on right now

2) Not-right-now ideas

3) Ideas to let go

Successful people don't let a "right now" idea stew for years. They use it or lose it. They are good at shelving ideas to be completed at a later date, and trashing ideas they choose not to accomplish.

However, even entrepreneurs who function at a high level of idea cultivation struggle with taking action on a consistent basis. And thus the balance struggle is born. How do you go from planning to action? When does the rubber meet the road?

There are ideas inside you right now that need to come to life. What ideas can you take action on right now? What ideas should be shelved for later use? What ideas should you ultimately let go of?

1) Right-Now Ideas

There are ideas you can accomplish right now or relatively soon. Accomplish these goals and tasks now. Set a new priority in your life to work on these ideas first.

I wrote a book last summer. It didn't take me years, and the idea didn't fester on the shelf for a decade. No. I brought the first draft to life in three weeks. In the book, *Volcanic Momentum*, I spoke at length about setting Destiny Goals. These types of goals are what you can do to make the world a better place. Your Destiny Goals are your actionable ideas to take your business to the next level, start a non-profit, or make strides to end homelessness in your local community.

As I wrote, I recognized that the book itself was a Destiny Goal and a great idea I could very quickly bring into the world, and so I did.

But it was also something I knew I had within me and could quickly create. I didn't hesitate, and I quickly and efficiently accomplished the goal.

Right-now ideas are actionable ideas you can do within the next few months or even the next few minutes. Maybe your Grandma needs just one thank-you card this holiday season to fill her with warmth and contentment. This is an example of an idea that is simple to act on but makes a world of difference by adding joy to another person's life.

Start to think about the goals you can accomplish right now, and go do them.

2) Not-Right-Now Ideas

You'll notice that I jump from right-now ideas to not-right-now ideas. There isn't a middle ground. It's not useful to keep good ideas in a holding pattern between "Yes I need to do that" and "I can't do it right away." This is the void where good ideas go to die.

Not-right-now ideas are your great ideas that can't be undertaken right away OR have other steps that need to be completed before they can become reality.

For example, my wife and I have plans to open a non-profit and adopt children. But these plans are not going to happen right away. Other financial and life goals need to be met first before we could even consider taking this on. Even though these are great ideas, they can't come to fruition right now and that's okay.

Your not-right-now ideas should be easy to label, but worth waiting on. These ideas are long-term goals to continue to work toward, but can't be accomplished any time soon. These are the ideas you either need to wait to complete or are unsure how they fit into your life plan.

The good news is these ideas give you something bigger to work toward. They answer the questions "What am I here for, why am I waking up every day, and what do I want my life to look like?"

Consider what your not-right-now ideas are and be okay with shelving them for completion later on.

3) Ideas to let go

Sometimes after a brainstorming session what you thought was the next best idea was absolute garbage. Sometimes ideas have to be attempted before you know whether it's fruitful. This is normal and a good thing. Just go with it. Other times, it's not easy to tell right away.

So how do you know whether an idea is good or bad? Follow these steps:

- The mom test: If your mom loves the idea, move on to the next step of executing the idea or shelving it for later use. If your mom doesn't like the idea, toss it out. If your mom laughs at the idea, get a new mom (just kidding). In all seriousness, the best way to feel out a new idea is to ask or tell it to one person. Talking about an idea out loud does two things: first, it forces you to describe the idea in a clear way, which will show you right away whether it makes sense or has potential, and then it gives you immediate feedback you can trust.

- Trust your gut and intuition. Discard any idea that feels off. If it's meant to be, it will come back. It's also important to note here that an idea might be bad because it's not right for you. Not all ideas have to be our ideas. Your best friend might have an idea that's perfect for you and vice versa. Get in the habit of sharing ideas whenever possible and don't feel that the burden of changing the world is on your shoulders. You are just one person who has the potential to make a difference, but it's not all on you (unless your name is Neo).

- Ask your customers or fans. One of the best ways to find out quickly if an idea is worth its weight in gold is to ask. If you get immediate negative feedback or, even worse, the crickets come out to play, you might be best served tossing the idea out with the bathwater.

- Is there market proof for the idea? Has someone else tried it before? If the idea isn't the most incredible idea you've ever had, chances are it's been thought of before, so why doesn't it already exist?

- Test out your idea in the real world, albeit in a limited way. If it's a book idea, write a blog first; if it's a big idea for community change, ask other members of the community for their feedback; if it's an idea for a new type of chair, build a prototype and let someone try it. Don't go all out for something that's untested.

- Even when you start an idea, you might not know for sure whether the idea is good or bad. Err on the side of experimentation, and be ready to pull the plug and pivot if it isn't working. A realistic mindset is important here. Give the idea the breathing room it needs to flesh itself out, but don't be afraid to move on if needed. Don't be a quitter, but don't get stuck either.

When you're ready, toss the bad ideas into the garbage and move on.

You could have ruminated on the garbage idea for years if you hadn't poured a dose of reality on it. Now, instead of letting an old idea die a slow, painful death, you can learn to move on from ineffective ideas early to keep things fresh and less painful.

The good thing is that yesterday's idea won't be as hard to let go of as an idea that's been percolating for years. Don't stew on one idea for too long. Master this cultivation process early. It's similar to liking a girl for years before you ever said one word to her. Big mistake! Don't get stuck on what could be before any actualization has taken place. Don't spend two years fawning on a girl who won't like you back.

There's nothing worse than shedding the light on your "brilliant" idea that's been in your head forever, only to find it won't work. I've had my fair share of experiences with this, as some ideas just won't work in the real world no matter how good they sound on paper.

I keep all of my ideas on a Trello board titled "Ideas." Exciting, right? It works for me. All of my ideas relate to writing blogs or books because that's where my head is most of the time. For example, here are some of my "bad" book ideas:

- Captain Nonconformity
- Disconnect to Connect
- The Problem with Science
- Dream Big: 51 Ideas to Dream Big and Make a Difference

Feel free to take any of these book ideas and do with them as you wish. They aren't good for me. The point is, if we are brainstorming and thinking of ideas on a constant basis, we are bound to have a few (or more than a few) duds. Hidden within those dud ideas are gems in the "not-right-now" pile, and I can't wait to bring them to fruition.

The sooner you can say no to a bad idea the more room you'll have for better ideas. Clear out the idea closet with some brainstorming magic and be ready to move forward with great ideas.

Mastering the Planning Stage

Brainstorming is a superpower. You may have never heard of Captain Brainstorm, but I am pretty sure she could beat both Thor and Iron Man in a battle royale. There is nothing as powerful for idea cultivation as breaking out the big guns and getting your brainstorm on.

My wife and I plan brainstorming sessions whenever our motivation is lacking and it gives us the boost we need to carry on. Friday night brainstorming sessions are a staple to kick bad energy to the curb and reinvigorate our drive for success and life-change.

Now, you don't have to go as far as brainstorming on date night, but you would do well to plan a session with someone close to you. Dreaming about what could be and then making plans to put your ideas into action might just be one of the best experiences you share with someone else.

Get your brainstorm on and make a list of all your ideas. This includes your goals, wants, desires, and plans. Think outside the box and get everything down on paper, whiteboard or Google doc. I can't emphasize enough how beneficial this is. If you haven't done this type of activity before, take a few minutes and try it now.

Did you do it?

Good. Now take those ideas and break them down into the types listed above. What ideas can you tackle now (in the next few months)? What ideas need time to grow? What ideas aren't worth a grain of salt?

On the following page I want you to list three ideas for each type. This will help get your mind thinking about ideas in this way so it will become a habit. Before long, you'll recognize the types of ideas as they come and will save boatloads of time.

BRAINSTORM YOUR IDEAS:

Right-now ideas:

Increase network.

share products, identify need

Create grand opening sermons.

Not-right-now ideas:

Trip around the world.

Buy a home

Travel interstate to meet people

Ideas that should be let go:

Taking Action on Your Ideas

Now it's time for my favorite question, how to take action. As entrepreneurs, we take action more often than most (because we rock). Still, taking the right action is a skill we need to fine tune. We struggle to take action in a way which doesn't leave us burnt out, exhausted, and unfulfilled. This is the balance point on which we must teeter effectively; being able to plan just enough, and then take major positive action on our ideas without crashing and burning.

First, we must believe in our ideas and the importance of bringing them to life. The world can be changed by ideas, whether those ideas are right-now ideas or ideas waiting on the right timing and resources.

Ever heard of the company FloodConcern?[1] FloodConcern has been tested against past events such as Hurricane Harvey to show that it could have been used to forecast flooding. The Silicon Valley company started with earthquakes and has since earned contracts with cities and private insurance companies. It's a tool that started with an idea, and now it's changing lives.

I know you know intrinsically that good ideas can change the world, but it's good to be reminded that you have the potential to do this as well. Do you think the person who dreamed up the plan to go to the Moon wasn't laughed at? And yet we achieved the impossible fifty years ago with primitive technology. We shouldn't have been able to do it, but we did.

Ideas need positive action behind them in order to come to life. Let's balance out the scale and take some action.

---

1   Clendaniel, Morgan, and Morgan Clendaniel. "World Changing Ideas 2019: 17 Winning Solutions That Could Save the Planet." Fast Company. April 08, 2019. Accessed June 08, 2019. https://www.fastcompany.com/90329204/world-changing-ideas-2019-17-winning-solutions-that-could-save-the-planet.

Break the Idea Down Into Baby Steps and do the First Step

You've brainstormed, determined your idea is brilliant, and now it's time to game plan. Yes! This is where balance between planning and action is found. This is the critical juncture—and where we often get lost.

Take one good right-now idea and break it down into manageable pieces.

If your goal is to grow your email list by 1000 subscribers in the next month, break it down into manageable tasks in order to take consistent action, such as:

1) Week one: Create a lead magnet for my website
2) Week two: Make a bonus opt-in for my high-performing blog posts
3) Week three: Run a book giveaway
4) Week four: Advertise my best converting lead magnet on Facebook

Start here and break down your idea into chunks that can be completed. Make sure these chunks are actionable tasks. This is the key difference. What you do NOT want to do is give yourself tasks that you can't complete, such as:

1) Week one: Get 10 subscribers
2) Week two: Get 100 subscribers
3) And so on…

This type of breakdown doesn't give you actionable steps to accomplish your goal. You might laugh at this type of breakdown, but I've seen companies and individuals do exactly this. Think about weight loss.

The goal is often to lose x amount of weight by a certain date, but the tasks within are usually to check your weight every day and hope the weight goes down. It doesn't work.

To take consistent positive action we have to break down the goal into actionable tasks that we can complete. Each item in the list needs to be accomplishable only by means of taking direct action.

Maybe by the end of the email task list above we don't have 1000 new subscribers. We might not hit our goal, but we would have learned a lot along the way, and maybe the next month we fill our time with tasks that we know will work instead of guessing.

We learn by doing. Only by starting will we know how to take the next step, and the next. True learning exists in the doing, not in reading an instruction manual all the way through.

What prevents us from taking the first step is fear. Fear in the form of:

- **Lost time:** We don't want to invest our time in a bad idea. Do the steps above and your idea is more than likely NOT a bad idea. Things might not work out but at the very least you will learn something. Remember, it's almost always better to err on the side of action and take a lesson from the school of hard knocks if need be.

- **Failure:** The fear of failure is huge and often the most limiting. We don't want to let others see us fall flat on our face. But this fear is misplaced. View failure as a building block to your next success. I've failed countless times and have often looked foolish, but every single time I've failed I've learned one more way not to do something. Use failure as a building block instead of a roadblock.

- **Change:** We are programmed to seek comfort, but growth does not occur in times of comfort. We need to shake off the notion that we truly want to be comfortable because deep down we don't. We don't want to be comfortable because in comfort we will eventually lose meaning and purpose. Purpose is the lifeblood of a life well lived.

Conquer these fears by taking that first step and experiencing new life. I want this so bad for you! I've seen the good that can come out of taking a deep breath and diving in head first.

Lives can be changed forever because you have the guts to do something most people only dream of by fulfilling your greater purpose.

Take Action Now

It's not enough to plan. In his book *The 15 Invaluable Laws of Growth: Live Them and Reach Your Potential,*[2] author and speaker John C. Maxwell shares the following advice:

> "What are we going to do? It's not enough to just plan, though planning is important. Both plan and action must go together. The plan creates the track. The action provides the traction. So anytime you have a goal but you think you won't be able to reach it, don't adjust the goal. Adjust the action steps."

Find success by taking action now instead of coming up with excuses why you can't get started.

List out the first five steps you need to take to make things happen. Ponder each of those steps. What challenges will you face?

---

2   Maxwell, John C. *The 15 Invaluable Laws of Growth: Live Them and Reach Your Potential.* New York: Center Street, 2014.

Get everything out on paper and get a feel for how things are going to go. Then, for each step, write out a completion date and get to work.

Now that you have the idea broken down into a process, take the first step this week. Don't wait for a later date. If you can't start on it right now then it's a not-right-now idea. Shelve the idea and pick a new right-now idea you can accomplish now.

This part is not an oversimplification of advice. We've all heard that we need to take the first step, but how often do we actually follow it? Not often enough.

Taking the first step and then the next takes courage, consistent energy, and time. Analyze your priorities and tackle what's important first, and then get to work. It's amazing how much energy can flow forth as soon as we start to work an idea. Momentum is created in minutes and we get locked in.

Taking consistent positive action is a mindset and process in which you stop making time for activities that won't move the needle. Do what needs to be done first to fulfill your obligations and responsibilities. With the time remaining, start checking off items on your to-do list. Make time to achieve your goals, and most importantly, continue to show up every day and spend time working towards your right-now idea.

Wrap Up

Entrepreneurs usually kick butt with planning and taking action, but there are times when analysis paralysis sets in or we find ourselves taking action without a guidepost. It's easy to get lost along the way if we aren't careful.

Make a consistent time to plan each week, each month, and each year.

Once you have a solid plan in place, take action. Don't get lost in the weeds of early results no matter how bad they might be. Push through and keep going. Find the balance point of consistent planning and take positive action on those plans.

Plan, take action, plan some more, take more action. Learning to switch back and forth will become easier in time, and your ideas will come to fruition, making way for bigger and better ideas and even more action. Change hats often and keep growing. You've got this.

PREPARATION VS. ACTION SELF-RATING

Do you spend most of your time planning and getting every-thing perfect or do you err on the side of action and just go with it? Where do you fall on the following scale? Mark your spot now.

At the end of the book you'll go back and take note of your responses to build your balance blueprint. If you tend toward action or preparation, circle that word. If you're good to go, check the box. If you are slightly toward action, tick some-where in between. If you are unsure, leave it blank for now but come back to it later. You'll do the same at the end of each balance-point chapter.

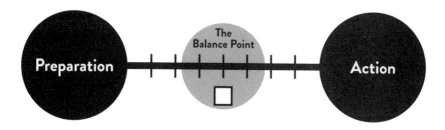

CHAPTER TWO

WORK VS. PLAY

"Once you have commitment, you need the
discipline and hard work to get you there."
—Haile Gebrselassie

"If you never did you should.
These things are fun, and fun is good."
—Dr. Seuss

Andrew is dominating ping pong with his friends at his 30th Birthday party.

"High-five partner!" He exclaimed to his wife as she finished off their opponent with a deft spin move.

"You're such a dork," she said as she high-fived him back.

Andrew leaned in to give Chloe a quick kiss. Something vibrated on the table between them. He snatched his phone off the table, reading a quick email with the subject "Urgent: read now."

Crap, he thought. I guess I need to get this.

He opened the email and scanned the first few sentences. His party mood drained away faster than his friend drained a cup of beer. His warehouse was shutting down. The warehouse was located across the country. It was eight on a Friday night for him, but the warehouse's workday was just ending and he might be able to catch them.

He dropped everything to go upstairs to his office. Over the next few hours he stared down at the party happening while he switched between email and talking on the phone. He watched his wife sit down partnerless beside the ping pong table and felt a deep pang of regret.

"Andrew, people are leaving!" Chloe said in hushed whisper through a cracked door. At long last he had arranged for his current orders to shift to another warehouse so they'd only be delayed by three days. Close call and crisis averted.

Andrew finally came downstairs just as the last stragglers were getting ready to leave. "Sorry guys, work emergency," he said apologetically.

"It's okay man." His friend said. "We enjoyed the party; we'll catch you next time."

With just the two of them left and the clock reading 3:00 AM, Chloe did her best to calm Andrew down by offering him a toast for just the two of them.

Andrew took the shot, said goodnight to Chloe, and sat down in front of the TV feeling exhausted.

Andrew awoke at noon the next day, in the midst of all the trash from the party and a hangover. He was so tired he never even made it upstairs. He stared around him at the scattered plastic cups, cold pizza, and ping pong balls. He rubbed his face knowing he needed to get to work and made a quick decision. He popped a few ibuprofen, drank a glass of water, and started cleaning up.

Over a home-cooked dinner that he had prepared for just the two of them, Andrew looked over at Chloe and said "Sorry for ditching the party Chlo', but I had to deal with the issue ASAP." Mid-sentence his phone chirped. He compulsively got up to check it, but thought better of it when he saw the look he was getting. Chloe stared at him.

"Are you going to answer that?" He took the phone, powered it down, and put it in a drawer.

Andrew might bail on friends for a work emergency, but he wouldn't bail on his lovely wife (not again, watching her sit partnerless had stung). He would dine with her and check his phone later on. It could wait. Hearing about his wife's day would not.

- -

Striking a balance between work and play is delicate at best, and dicey at worst.

My wife Miranda and I spent January through March of 2019 in Thailand. It was the first time we've ever done such a long international trip away from home. We LOVED it. There were always new sights to see, new people to interact with, and new foods to try.

We wanted to experience all Thailand had to offer, and we could have. If we let ourselves, we could have easily spent every day playing instead of working. We could have gone somewhere different to eat for each meal over the two months we were there. Except we knew that in order to keep doing trips like this in the near future, we needed to stay vigilant with our work efforts. We needed to continue to build on our income streams at every level in order to keep the digital nomad lifestyle going.

Striking this balance is key to maintaining your stride as an entrepreneur. If you can master the planning and action balance, the next step is to figure out how much time to spend working vs. playing, because guess what? YOU get to choose!

You, and only you, get to pick what you do with your time. This is true of any individual, but when the hours in the day are entirely your responsibility to fill up, managing that time can seem daunting. So much time can be liberating and almost intoxicating, but it can also be poisonous. The level of discipline needed to maintain balance is high but not impossible to reach.

Over the last few years of working as an authorpreneur I've learned that the best way to maintain discipline is to change pace often by going to different places to work, getting up really early one day or staying up late another day. The more I try, the more I can see what works and what doesn't. When something works, I do my best to formulate it as a habit (for example, doing one quick task first even if it's an annoying one). Then I stack other positive habits around that one. Sounds simple, but we have to be on the lookout for new ways to get work done and get it done well.

The bottom line? Work is important. The work we do has the potential to change lives and build a better future, and if we do it well, we can make money too.

But equally important? Taking a break and having fun so we can be in it for the long haul, doing what we do and building on our successes.

Below I explain fifteen work/life balance tips you can begin to use today. I suggest implementing any in your life that you find effective and valuable.

To find a balance between work and play, utilize any or all of the following tricks of the trade. You'll find these tips particularly useful for time management and each one can be applied to normal daily life to find balance.

Work vs. Play Tip #1: Work Whenever There isn't Much Else to do

This one is easy to say, and tough to implement. It's useful to take advantage of times when there isn't much going on. Whether it's pouring down rain or you are stuck in an airport for twelve hours, find a way to get stuff done. This will allow you that much more freedom to play on the nice days and have fun when you get to your final destination.

Think about what time can be gained that is otherwise wasted.

Try reading on your Kindle app while waiting in a line. Do talk to other people if the mood strikes, but otherwise waiting in line could be considered wasted time. Fill that with reading instead.

Don't counterbalance and fill every waking moment of "free" time with activity. I'm not one of those who ascribe to this type of lifestyle. Thoughtful ponderings and casual human interaction are important for overall growth as well. Mix it up and find what works for you.

Work vs. Play Tip #2: Start, You Aren't Missing Out

When you are lacking motivation and you'd much rather just go outside, sit down and get to work instead. For me, this works like a charm. I can still trick myself into thinking I'll only work for a bit, but every time I open my laptop it turns into a two to three-hour work session.

This step is easier now since we just recently had an amazing Thailand adventure. We returned to stunningly beautiful North Carolina weather. I look outside and I'd much rather be out there than working on my computer, but having a recent major experience makes missing out on a nice day seem less important.

Start, knowing that you aren't really missing out on anything as the work you are doing is important.

Work vs. Play Tip #3: Be Intentional

Set aside time every day for the most important tasks for your business. This will allow you to be guilt free when you do something fun in the evening after a long day of work. It's hard to find consistent motivation in work, even if you love what you do. For most of us, we will hit a wall and need a break.

Intentionality is the lifeblood of every successful entrepreneur. Know what you plan to accomplish each week, month, and year, and set your tasks accordingly.

What I've been learning to do is to wake up every day with at least one idea in mind of a task I want to get done. Often it's more than one task, but the one I get done is the most important to move forward in my goals. It's hard not to get caught up in the busyness of tasks that demand attention, and being intentional about our daily tasks is how we move forward effectively.

Prioritize doing what needs to be done for your work. Put time into tasks and items that demand attention, but don't forget to be intentional with your time for both work and play.

Work vs. Play Tip #4: Get a Flexible Job

For me, as soon as I got into the world of online freelancing and passive income I was hooked. It's been said entrepreneurs are the only people that will work eighty hours to avoid working forty. This couldn't be more true. I find value in making my own schedule, determining my own working hours, and keeping myself accountable. Some days are challenging, but having flexibility makes it all worth it.

After Thailand, we then went to Maine to see my parents. A week later we went to Pennsylvania to see other family members. The freedom to travel in this way is not possible with a 9-to-5 job with minimal paid time off.

The more flexible your working situation, the more time you will have for other pursuits, such as enhancing your skills for the job you already have. The more we make ourselves invaluable assets, the more leeway we have to strike the work/life balance we want.

I'm never going back to a less flexible job if I can help it, and it's because of the freedom to decide what to do with my time. I can take a day and work on my next book, or take the day to freelance and work for clients. I can choose how much time to work and how much time to play. Sometimes this can add pressure, feelings of guilt, and other challenges, but it's much easier to handle than limited vacation time, being on-call overnight, or working a full year for the chance at a small raise.

Maybe you are an aspiring entrepreneur who's reading this book in the hopes of finding tips to become what you were born to be. I say to you: Go get it! Make a plan and reach for flexibility. Work a side hustle until it becomes a full-time gig. Or just take a risk now and use your savings to float you while you work like crazy to light up the world.

Working as a full-time entrepreneur is one of the best feelings. If you aren't already choosing how to use your time each day, find a way to get there.

Work vs. Play Tip #5: Love What You do

"If you love the work you do, you won't work a day in your life." Author and speaker John C. Maxwell says this often. I love it, and I'm trying to live it. If you find something you are truly passionate about, it no longer feels like work; it becomes a calling and something you would probably do for free. With my writing I am getting closer, but I still have a long way to go.

I think we all have the ability to find work that we are passionate about. It won't happen right away, but it's worth it when you find it. When I write and get in the flow, the world flies by around me and I don't even think about anything else. There is something out there uniquely designed for you and your passions and abilities. Maybe you already know what it is.

Work vs. Play Tip #6: Find Purpose in Your Work

In his book *Great at Work: How Top Performers Work Less and Achieve More*[3], Morten Hansen, management professor at the University of California, Berkeley, shares that purpose trumps passion when it comes to productivity and meaning.

When answering the prompt, "What I do at work makes a strong contribution to society beyond making money," only 17% of the 5000 employees surveyed agreed. These employees also had the highest performance rankings with their bosses.

---

3   Hansen, Morten. *GREAT AT WORK: How Top Performers Do Less, Work Better, and Achieve More*. S.l.: SIMON & SCHUSTER, 2019.

Hansen further found interesting results when grouping employees into four separate categories:

1) **Low passion and low purpose:** These folks were rated at the bottom 10% of performance by their bosses. No surprise here.

2) **High Passion and High Purpose:** These employees rated in top 80th percentile for performance. Again, no surprise here. Folks who love what they do AND feel their purpose is fulfilled are the stars of the company.

3) **High Passion and Low Purpose:** The results of the study are no longer obvious. Hansen found that these employees fell in the 20th percentile of job performance. These people love what they do and have a high level of passion, but they don't know why they do it.

4) **Low Passion and High Purpose:** These folks are shockingly in the 64th percentile of high performing employees. This means that one can be dulled by the work, but if it has a high level of meaning people will still perform well. Fascinating.

We should consider finding purpose in what we do. It will lead us to better results and higher levels of performance.

Purpose trumps passion in the realm of efficiency, but we still would do well to mix in passion too.

We will go into these concepts in greater depth in chapter four when we discuss purpose vs. passion.

Work vs. Play Tip #7: Schedule Fun Activities

If you don't make time to have fun, it might not happen. Every entrepreneur who finds valuable work can enjoy it so much they forget to have fun. If you don't take a break and proactively schedule fun activities, you'll face burnout and an eventual lack of interest in your subject matter.

Learn to let go and to make time for fun. This applies not only to those with a lot of time on their hands, but to people with full schedules too. We all need to schedule time to take a chill pill once in a while and relax.

And remember too, the fun thing doesn't have to be momentous. It could be as simple as taking a night off to go to the movies, ordering take out, or taking a walk.

The only thing you need to do is to schedule it and make sure it happens. Be intentional about carving out time for play.

Work vs. Play Tip #8: Take a Wednesday Off

Don't forget that you are in charge of your schedule. If you find that you are overworked and burning out by the middle of the week, stop working and take the day off, for Pete's sake. If you find that you are putting too much focus on work, stop for a change and tune out all other distractions.

Entrepreneurs crash and burn quickly. I've ridden the roller coaster and it ain't pretty. I'm gung ho for work on a Monday and Tuesday but by hump day I'm toast. I wake up unable to get anything worthwhile accomplished.

And instead of just calling it, what do I do? I try to power through, end up getting distracted, and put out subpar work that took me far too long to do. Not good.

I've learned that some days aren't going to be successful. Some days won't provide you the creative mojo you need. Instead, go for a walk and take the day to read. Give your mind a break from the constant stress of production and feed it content related to your niche.

Your day off doesn't have to be a Wednesday, Saturday, or Sunday. Maybe you like to work hard for four days and take a long weekend. The point is to find what works for you and don't stop experimenting until you find the sweet spot.

Work vs. Play Tip #9: Take a Working Trip to a Foreign Country

What better way to combine both work and play than taking a work trip to another country?

Our trip to Thailand this past year was fantastic for breaking out and doing new things. It sparked my creativity and at times it was hard to stop writing because I had so much in my head to get out.

Creativity lives and breathes when our brain is jazzed up by seeing and experiencing new things. Sure, it can be exhausting to travel and figure out a new routine, but the benefits far outweigh these inconveniences.

I wrote this very book whilst working at over thirty cafes, coffee shops, and coworking spaces in a foreign country. Compare that to working out of my home office, the same Barnes and Noble table, and the occasional Starbucks, and it's no wonder the words burst forth onto the page.

Beyond just work, consider how easy it is to take a break and experience new things. In Chiang Mai, Thailand alone my wife and I must have eaten at over fifty unique restaurants! We would often take a two-hour break, grab some food we hadn't tried before, and then get back to work. It was the perfect mix of adventure and motivation to keep working as much as possible.

Be warned though! Travel is addictive and Miranda and I are already planning our next trips to see other interesting places.

I don't want to live with a single regret, and I don't want you to either. Find a way to take a trip, just once, and your eyes will be open to new possibilities. We aren't meant to stick to one thing our whole lives. We are meant for more.

Work vs. Play Tip #10: Power Down Your Mobile Device

One of the worst things you can do when you finally decide to have fun is to keep the phone on. Don't let the phone become an unshakeable tether to your work life. If you can leave it behind, do so. If you have to keep it with you "just in case," shut it off or put it in airplane mode.

Being disconnected for even a few hours has healing powers. The average person looks at their phone 110 times a day[4] and spends 23 days per year[5] glued to their smartphone. Have you ever felt the phantom buzz, only to find out your phone isn't even in your pocket? It's at those times I think it might be time to leave the phone in the other room and disconnect completely.

---

4   Woollaston, Victoria. "How Often Do You Check Your Phone? The Average Person Does It 110 times a DAY (and Every 6 Seconds in the Evening)." Daily Mail Online. October 08, 2013. Accessed June 08, 2019. http://www.dailymail .co.uk/sciencetech/article-2449632/How-check-phone-The-average-person -does-110-times-DAY-6-seconds-evening.html.

5   "23 Days a Year Spent on Your Phone." 23 Days a Year Spent on Your Phone -. Accessed June 08, 2019. http://www.mobilestatistics.com/mobile-news/23 -days-a-year-spent-on-your-phone.aspx.

We didn't have cell phone coverage while we were on our trip. We could have put in local sim cards and had access to the local 4G network, but we chose not to. Instead our phones only worked when on WiFi.

Guess what? We were fine. We didn't need to be connected 24/7 with access at all times. Sure, there were times when Miranda and I were in separate places and I wasn't able to touch base with her, but such occurrences were few and far between. Plus, there's WiFi everywhere in Chiang Mai so it worked out.

Tuck your phone away and get off the grid every once in a while. Trust me, it's all good.

Work vs. Play Tip #11: Check Email Only Once or Twice Per Day

This is one of those tips you know you should probably do but it's almost impossible in practice. A few practical suggestions:

1) Be intentional about checking your email. Too often I open up my email on my phone with no intention of responding. Am I saving any time by doing this, or are those minutes wasted?

2) Don't connect your email accounts to your phone. You probably don't need to have access to it 24/7. Instead, check email only when you are on your laptop and are capable of responding in depth.

3) Remember to set an away message whenever you might take longer to respond to inquiries. You should still do your best to respond in a timely manner, but with an away message, people won't feel like you are leaving them hanging.

4) Filter your email. If you use Gmail, you can set filters on

incoming messages to establish a level of priority. If you have a few top-level clients you want to respond to right away, set up a specific inbox just for them and get notified when you receive their emails. Put all other emails into a separate folder you know is less of a priority. It might not seem fair, but we don't get ahead by doing what's fair, we get ahead by doing what works for us. Some people might have to wait for a response and that's okay.

Mastering email is a challenging process. If you still can't get it right and feel constantly overwhelmed, you might want to consider hiring a VA (virtual assistant) to sort email for you or to respond in your name when appropriate. Get creative and don't feel stuck with email. There are always creative solutions right around the corner.

Work vs. Play Tip #12: Work During Your Peak Hours of Focus

What times of the day are you at your best? At what time does it feel like pulling teeth to even open up your email, let alone trying to respond in a coherent manner?

Work when you have the best chance to get into the flow and do solid work. When I first wake up in the morning I am NOT with it. I can barely function right off the bat. I do much better work in the afternoons or evenings when the food, coffee, and a good workout kick in.

Find a time of day that works for you and schedule your day to utilize your peak focus time. Get your best work done when you know you'll get your best work done.

Work vs. Play Tip #13: Don't Neglect Health and Wellness

On the grand adventure to finding balance as an entrepreneur, health and wellness often get tanked. We stop drinking enough water, stop finding the time to work out, and don't even get me started on the food choices.

Make today the day you reset and make better decisions in this area. There are countless books you can read on the subject, but you probably know what to do. Start doing it. Remember, you are in this for the long haul. Choose wellness.

Chapter nine is hustle vs. health so keep reading for more on this subject.

Work vs. Play Tip #14: Multitask Only When it Makes Sense

Multitasking is not how we get ahead. If we multitask too much we risk getting behind and not using our brain to its fullest capacity. A study done by the University of London[6] found that multitasking's effect on the brain is akin to staying up all night.

The American Psychological Association shows that multitasking is actually less efficient because it takes additional time to switch between tasks and it ends up taking a toll on productivity.[7]

---

6   Janssen, Gould, Li, Brumby, and Cox. "Integrating Knowledge of Multitasking and Interruptions across Different Perspectives and Research Methods." Integrating Knowledge of Multitasking and Interruptions across Different Perspectives and Research Methods. July 01, 2015. Accessed June 08, 2019. http://discovery.ucl.ac.uk/1465496/.

7   "Multitasking: Switching Costs." American Psychological Association. Accessed June 08, 2019. https://www.apa.org/research/action/multitask.

Next time you think about watching YouTube or checking emails at the same time as spending time with your kids, consider focusing on one important activity at a time.

On the other side of the coin, here are some activities fantastic for productivity that you can do simultaneously:

- Walking or driving while listening to audiobooks.
- Reading while listening to calming music.
- Make a phone call while doing the dishes.
- Exercise while watching the latest episode of your favorite TV series (it's much better for you than watching whilst sitting down).
- Work while watching sports. Most of the time spent in sports games (especially baseball) is spent on things other than playing (like commercials). Get some additional work done when your favorite team isn't up to bat.

Pick tasks that make sense to do together and won't collide. Put time, energy, and your undivided focus into the big things that really matter.

Work vs. Play Tip #15: Don't Forget, You Run the Show

This one is easy to forget. It's easy to get locked into habits and into doing things just because it's the way you do them. Don't forget to question why you do things the way you do, especially if you are finding less and less passion for what you do.

As an entrepreneur, life can still get stressful, difficult, and overwhelming. Don't think that a life away from the corporate world is easy; entrepreneurship comes with its own challenges.

Remember you have the authority to dictate your schedule. Build your day around what works for you and be the boss.

Use these tips today to begin to master the art of balance. When you can seamlessly slip from work to play as effortlessly as a dolphin dives into cool crisp waters, you will know you are close to achieving the work-life balance everyone so desperately wants.

Be intentional above all else. See where you need to improve and make a concerted effort to do so. It will take time but it's well worth it.

WORK VS. PLAY SELF-RATING

Do you work all the time or do you always choose to play? Mark the spot where you tend to lean most or check the box if you have balance in this area. We will revisit these later on so you can build your personal balance blueprint.

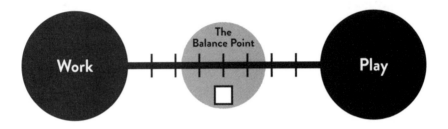

CHAPTER THREE
YES VS. NO

"He who is not courageous enough to take risks will accomplish nothing in life."
—Muhammad Ali

"Adopt the pace of nature: her secret is patience."
—Ralph Waldo Emerson

"I moved over 5000 units last month alone," said Jeremy.

Andrew's eyes glazed over. He was sitting in the back of the room at the latest Amazon meetup downtown, and was listening to success story after success story.

"10,000 sold for me," said Blair.

Another eye roll. He loved getting motivated but was getting sick of not getting any major wins himself.

When he was finally called on to give an update he shrugged and mumbled something about just getting started, but moving 500 last month.

After an agonizing hour of success stories the meeting finally came to an end. Andrew packed up, got ready to leave, but was stopped by Jeremy before he made it out.

"Did you try it yet?" Jeremy said with a wink.

"No, I've been waiting for you to get caught so I can laugh at you," Andrew said as he punched Jeremy on the arm.

"Nah man you know I'm not going to get caught; it's totally legit."

For months now Jeremy had been trying to get Andrew to try out this new website called GetProductReviewsNow to add legitimacy to his Amazon listings. The site wasn't clear on how it did what it did, but Jeremy had been getting solid verified reviews as well as increased sales for months now.

"Can you send it to me again? I'll check it out."

Andrew left the meeting with a nagging feeling that he was headed down a dark path. When he got home he opened his account and saw four sales for the day. A pittance. He was about to snap his laptop shut out of defiance, but instead loaded up the site Jeremy mentioned and bit the bullet. It was a big risk but he had to move his business forward.

About a month later his sales were increasing, and things were looking up. He was thrilled! Until one day he sat down at his desk and...

"Your Amazon account has been terminated effective immediately."

Andrew stared at his screen with abject horror.

He put his head down on the desk. His breathing came in short gasps and he could feel the tears coming as his emotions bubbled to the surface.

With a simple email, his major source of income was gone, and there was likely nothing he could do about it.

He checked again to be sure. Yep, the same words stuck out like a knife to his heart... "effective immediately."

Everything he had built in the past two years was crumbling down around him. He was panicking and didn't know where to turn. He knew he shouldn't have listened to Jeremy. This shortcut had cost him big this time.

He could picture the little voice in his head dancing and gloating because he was right. He shouldn't have taken this chance, it was far too risky. But the rewards made it worth it! … Or so he thought.

As panic set in, Andrew tried to slow his breathing. He knew he was freaking out and he couldn't help it. He had wavered into shortcuts and had hit the easy button one too many times.

Buying reviews for his product… How could he have been so STUPID!? He could feel the self-anger rising and intensifying so he stepped out of his office and sat down in the living room.

What had seemed like a great opportunity now seemed like the biggest mistake of his life. He had been persuaded to take this "chance of a lifetime" and been duped. He had dropped the ball once and now it was all over. He dropped his head into his lap and sobbed uncontrollably until Chloe came home, wiped his eyes, and held him like a mother holds a babe. He was utterly grateful, but he couldn't even muster the coherent thoughts needed to utter a quick "Thank you."

Andrew was defeated and in trouble.

A few weeks later Andrew went for what was now becoming a regular afternoon jog. He left a scribbled note on the counter saying he wouldn't be back until late. He planned to run until his feet wouldn't allow him one more step.

The tears, denial, and anger of the last few weeks had been diminishing as he consistently pounded the pavement, the new outlet for his rage. He imagined the ground dipping in with every step and sending him flying along. His mood had boosted tenfold of late, even though his shins were on fire most of the time. No matter.

Andrew had been back and forth with Amazon support over the last few weeks, and had finally been allowed to reopen his account, but with limitations and a probationary period. He would have to be much more careful with any new "opportunity."

To take advantage of his second chance he wrote *"Are you willing to lose everything?"* on the top of his office whiteboard.

When faced with an unclear and risky scenario and unsure if he should say yes or no, Andrew would ask himself this question before letting the Jeremys of the world convince him to take a risk.

- -

The struggle to find the balance point of yes vs. no is magnified as an entrepreneur. In most cases, you have no one to stand behind but yourself. You don't have anyone else to blame or rely on for support if the risk of the yes turns out to be too great. It's your business and you are responsible for it.

Say yes to too many opportunities and you won't have time to finish anything you start.

Say no to everything and your growth will stymie.

There is always going to be a risk associated with living an entrepreneurial lifestyle. It's a risk whether we say yes or no. Sometimes saying "no" is a bigger risk because we might be missing out on a great opportunity.

No matter which avenue you take as an entrepreneur, there are going to be risks involved that you'll have to deal with along the way. The better we can become at striking a solid balance early on, the more money we will make and the more secure we can feel with our choices.

So how do we do this? How do we strike a perfect balance between knowing when to jump and when to pass up an opportunity? How do we know when to say yes and when to run away?

The key is in asking tough questions from the start about the potential risks and rewards involved, whether the opportunity fits our current activities and projects, and if we are going to enjoy it. Be intentional about your decisions with these specific questions:

1) Do I have more to gain or more to lose by stepping through this door?

2) Is this a shiny new distraction or brand-new territory for me?

3) Is this new opportunity legit, or does it sound too good to be true?

4) Am I willing to risk everything I have for the chance at success?

Do I have more to gain or more to lose by stepping through this door?

This question is tough because we don't often know the reward potential, but often have a pretty good idea what we have to lose. If Andrew had asked himself this question when he considered purchasing reviews he would have been able to see that he had much more to lose than to gain.

Saying yes to this opportunity cost him dearly, and it happens all the time in real life too. I constantly hear about people who got their account terminated on Amazon just because they were trying to make a quick buck. If you are in it for the long haul as an entrepreneur you won't chase the quick wins served by risky tactics.

But we can't play it too safe either. We might have a lot to gain by going in a new direction, but since it is an unknown we don't know for sure whether it's a good idea.

I've always erred on the side of playing it safe online. This has cost time as there were tricks and tactics I was not employing that were okay. The positive is that I haven't gotten into trouble, but neither have things quickly taken off.

For example, many of my online friends and coworkers sell t-shirts on Amazon for quite a bit of money. I have heard reports of Amazon banning accounts for copyright infringement by the account holders. Some of the banned include well-meaning folks who took one too many risks or just made an honest mistake. It's still copyright infringement, but when you are trying to grow your business mistakes do occur. Grow too fast and take too many risks and you open up the door for headaches.

Uploading unique designs and checking your title for copyrighted phrases is standard safe practice, but looking up every word you are putting in your title can be time consuming. I know of people who skip this step and upload and hope their designs don't get flagged.

People who skip a copyright check are able to upload more designs than people who take their time. They are saying yes to the risk of copyright infringement out of ignorance for the chance at a quick buck. In this case, they know they aren't doing their due diligence, and are putting their accounts at risk. There are people out there who do find success by living and operating in a perpetual gray area. I don't recommend this approach to doing business. We must choose to do better as entrepreneurs seeking balance.

There will always be unknowns when it comes to deciding on new opportunities, but we need to be intentional about making the best decisions for our business.

Do you have more to lose or more to gain? Have you looked into the potential ramifications? Is there anyone you can reach out to and ask for clarity? Remember to ask these questions when something seems off and answer honestly. If things are going well for you, you might want to be a touch more careful. If you don't have much to lose, then maybe a little risk is worth it. It's up to you.

If an opportunity is ringing alarm bells in your subconscious or you are getting bad vibes when you get ready to say yes, say no instead. Stay clear of black-hat tactics and shady business opportunities and take the right kinds of risks.

Is this a shiny new distraction or brand-new territory for me?

Is what you are jumping into brand new? Do you know enough about it to make an accurate and informed decision on the risk potential? This is key! Your car will still be towed even if you "didn't know" it was a tow-away zone. You'll pay the fine regardless of your intent.

I've found that building a platform of specific skills and abilities has served me well over the past few years. Instead of chasing every shiny object and new idea that came my way, I've been saying no quite a bit and learning to only say yes to opportunities that augment my current business. I don't take on new responsibilities or pursue new opportunities without extreme consideration of whether it will help me grow or end up hindering my progress.

I don't like the feeling of missing out. Nobody likes FOMO. But sometimes we have to miss out on good opportunities so we can be available for great ones.

If the open door is brand new, and you have the wingspan to take it on, by all means do so. But if you are strapped for time, or just getting by with your current obligations, it might be a more viable option to say no.

If you can easily take it on and it makes sense to do so, go ahead. If you are basing every decision on building a base platform of skills, it's hard to lose. If the new direction complements several other areas at once, all the more reason to do it.

Beware of shiny new objects that don't directly relate to anything you are currently set up to do. They will drain time and energy better spent working on your current tasks, goals, and dreams.

Is this new opportunity legit, or does it sound too good to be true?

Sometimes we throw blinders up without even realizing it. Recently I read an article about Singapore endorsing a new cryptocurrency. It promised that if you jumped on it now you'd stand to make a lot of money.

Granted, it's pretty obvious now this was a scam, but it amazes me how money can turn off certain filters. I was ready to invest money right away if it meant capitalizing on this fantastic opportunity. Talk about being a sucker.

I know that you are a careful entrepreneur, and wouldn't be caught dead falling for something like this, but trust me when I say that we can and will look at the world with rose-colored glasses if the potential reward is just right.

Ask this question before running off and spending thousands on Singaporean Bitcoins.

Am I willing to risk everything I have for the chance at success?

This is the question for those life-altering decisions that come around from time to time. When Miranda and I first moved down south to Georgia and started a brand-new life working at a retirement community, it felt like a huge risk. We left behind friends and family and our jobs for a new start in a brand-new place.

It was scary, but we did it because we were willing to risk failing and falling flat on our faces. If faced with the same scenario now we'd say no because we have a lot more to lose with our current businesses and projects. We couldn't afford to neglect our responsibilities, and of course, we love what we do right now.

Are you at a point in your life where you are willing to risk it all? Are you willing to lose family time, your life savings, or your entire business if something doesn't pan out the way it should? This is a question only you can answer, but sometimes the most wonderful moments in our lives exist because we took a chance and ran with it.

This question applies to both yes and no. Don't say no to the big opportunity due to fear of failure, lack of initiative, or because you don't want to bet on yourself. Don't say yes just because it sounds like the next big thing and it has the potential to bring you health and happiness.

Be mindful of the reasons you are saying yes or no and be confident in your decision. We don't often know the ripple effects one bad decision could cause and thus the reason for intentional and mindful decisions.

Start with these questions in order to find balance with yes vs. no. Err on the side with which you are unfamiliar, especially if you are unsure where or how to start. Start somewhere, friend.

If you don't take big risks, change tactics and go for something big. Become a yes man/woman and take on new things. Experience growth by putting yourself out there and trying out new opportunities. Stop playing it safe and say yes to the next opportunity you are presented with (as long as it isn't shady or involves unnecessary risk).

If you find yourself picking up the pieces after yet another failed business attempt, spend time assessing your practices and habits and say no for the time being. Take a new, less risky road to grow into a better version of yourself that will find success. It doesn't have to happen overnight, and growth takes time. Don't beat yourself up when you don't get it right the first time.

We will often find the greatest growth in doing things outside our comfort zone. Spend each day pushing towards your growth and you will find great success.

YES VS. NO SELF-RATING

Do you say yes to every shiny object or do you avoid trying new things? Mark the spot where you tend to lean or check the box if you have balance in this area. We will revisit these later on so you can build your personal balance blueprint.

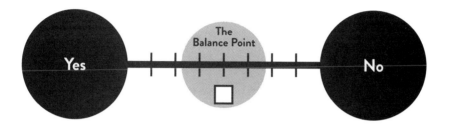

CHAPTER FOUR
PURPOSE VS. PASSION

"The purpose of human life is to serve, and to show compassion and the will to help others."
—Albert Schweitzer

"Passion is one great force that unleashes creativity, because if you're passionate about something, then you're more willing to take risks."
—Yo-Yo Ma

Andrew's pocket buzzed. When he saw who it was calling him he picked up right away.

"Hey Andrew!" Said Emily, Andrew's best friend growing up.

"Hey there sis," Andrew said with a grin. He always enjoyed catching up and chatting with Emily, even if he was trying to finish editing his latest video for his YouTube channel. "Did you catch the Bulls game last night?"

"Listen, not a lot of time to chat here, but was wondering if you could help her again?" Emily said.

Andrew sighed. He wouldn't be catching up after all, he would be doing his sworn duty instead. "Yeah, you got it. Did you tell her to hit the on button?" Andrew said.

"Yep! Seems like she messed it up real good this time," Emily said with a forced laugh. "You're the best. I appreciate you."

"I'll get right on it," Andrew said and hung up the phone. One disadvantage of living in your childhood hometown? Your best friend's grandmother lived nearby and was horrible with TVs.

Andrew got dressed and headed on over to Doris's house to see what he could do.

"Hey Doris, it's Andrew," he said through the cracked door after hitting the doorbell.

"Oh little Andy! Emily said you'd be here. You don't know how much I appreciate this," Doris said as she shuffled Andrew into the living room.

Andrew cringed at the sound of his least favorite nickname and went straight to the TV to start troubleshooting. He noticed several items unplugged and in disarray. Oh man… He had his work cut out for him.

As Doris continued to mumble things like, "I promise I don't know what I did," "Thank you for coming all the way over here," and "I was just about to make cookies would you like some?" Andrew got the TV set up and ready to go. He instructed Doris in the exact steps to fix the problem the next time, but he knew he'd be back.

Andrew couldn't stop smiling all the short drive home. He had quit his day job and built his business from the ground up, and yet these accomplishments paled in comparison to the joy of helping out Grandma Doris.

Andrew journaled his thoughts and pondered how to discover more moments like the one he had tonight.

He sent a quick text off to Emily saying, "Tell Doris thanks for the cookies! I'm available to help whenever she needs, just tell her to stop unplugging things ;)."

He got a quick reply that read, "Okay will do, thanks again Andrew! ☺."

Andrew leaned back in his chair and reached for another oatmeal-raisin cookie. He hadn't touched his overflowing inbox yet, but this reward made the prospect much sweeter.

- -

"I am Loki of Asgard, and I am burdened with glorious purpose."
—Loki Odinson

Most of us don't have as clear a purpose as the God of Mischief from the Marvel Cinematic Universe. Instead, we have all probably, at some point or another, looked up to the stars, to the vast universe that exists just beyond our understanding, and wondered, "What am I doing with my life? What is this all for? What purpose am I fulfilling in my life?"

I've had these exact thoughts, and I'm guessing you have too.

The problem is that there isn't a perfect answer. No one can give a perfect answer for you and your unique situation. Everyone has hidden struggles and battles raging in their hearts and internal struggles they must contend with. Life is an unpredictable, joyous mess.

The struggle between purpose and passion is subtle but important. We can't do a great job if we don't love what we do, and if what we love has no greater purpose, then it's meaningless. Swinging too far in either direction causes our lives to be devoid of meaning or joy.

It's of the utmost importance that you discover the job, career, or business that fills you with passion each day, and also fulfills a greater purpose.

In this chapter I will give you tools to question your purpose and passion in order to find a way to merge the two. I want you to discover the power of living the best of both worlds. Both purpose and passion are forces for good. Each will leave you empty without the other. It's imperative for long-term sustainability to get this right.

To find balance between purpose and passion, you must take a step back and take stock of your current life. We all have to decide what to do with our lives. We can live a life of no regrets or find ourselves disappointed in our later years. It's a choice worth pondering and intentionally figuring out.

Taking action toward a clouded future is hard, but these next few pages will help you to find positive direction and clarify your values.

These questions are perfect for anyone stuck in a job they hate, a college student with little direction, or the entrepreneur who has everything but still feels like they have nothing.

Keep in mind, your answers may change over time. We may find ourselves in a business we used to love, but now we can't wait until the end of the day so we can go do something else.

The first step is to take positive action steps towards your goal of determining your balance point between purpose and passion.

Question 1: What Would I do if I Could do Anything?

This question is one of my favorites to ask. It breaks us outside of the box for a hot minute. It gives us a chance to dream. It allows us to see what could be in a world where we too often hear "should be" or "can't be."

When you ask this question, don't limit your thinking by the parameters of your current circumstances. Brainstorm a list of anything and everything you would like to do with your life. Every entrepreneur is already a little bit outside the box. Use this to your advantage.

One effective exercise is to build a list of fifty life goals for yourself. Break it down this way (as Mark Matteson does in his book on mastering productivity *It's About Time*[8]):

- What are ten things I would like to *do*? (Examples: Write twenty-five books, sell a business for $10 million, compete in a hot-pepper eating challenge and win.)

- What are ten things I would like to *see*? (Examples: The Pyramids, my daughter's wedding, the ocean from my screened-in porch.)

- What are ten things I would like to *be*? (Examples: An international speaker, a winner of the Nobel Peace Prize, a screenwriter for Disney/Pixar.)

- What are ten fun things I want to *do*? (Examples: Travel to outer space, cliff dive in Bermuda, win a poker tournament and qualify for the World Series of Poker.)

- What are ten things I would like to *share* with the world? (Examples: I want my children to have a love for reading, I want to become a local legend beekeeper, I want to direct an indie film picked up by Netflix.)

Get to fifty goals and your eyes open up to the possibilities within your life. You'll see that life has so much more potential than you ever thought possible.

---

8   Matteson, Mark. *It's About Time: How to Get Twice as Much Done in Half the Time and Enjoy Balance and Peace of Mind!* Ugly Dog Publishing, 2014.

Question 2: If I Could Only Accomplish One More Thing in My Life What Would it Be?

This question follows in the footsteps of the big dreaming question before it. We don't know how much time we have left. A bus could hit us while walking to work, or we might get sick and have only a few months left to live. Forgive the morbidity here. The point is, we don't know how many days we have to do what we want to do. We could spend our lives just outside of the sweet spot and fulfill neither passion nor purpose, and never get the chance to find fulfillment. Some of us go our whole lives without stopping to ask if we are living with no regrets.

At some point there will be no tomorrow. If you knew you would die tomorrow, what would you do today?

I know it's tough to think about since we know we likely have plenty of time to accomplish our goals. The premise here is we shouldn't take any time for granted. We can't let our assumed amount of time prevent us from using our time wisely now.

In order to push forward and fulfill our true purpose we need to act now, before it's too late.

For example, if you set a deadline for a work project you're likely to get it done on or near that date. If the project has an open-ended timeline it will usually take until the end to finish. Get used to setting tight deadlines for your most important projects and focus on them until completion. It's the best way to live a life of no regrets and one "burdened with glorious purpose."

Question 3: Do I Have Any Regrets?

Regret is a fickle thing. It creeps up on us just when we can't do anything to change it. But when we notice regret, it can be used as a superpower for future actions. What in your life do you wish could be different?

Regrets are the greatest catalysts to future growth, if we so choose.

I regret spending most of my life up until the age of twenty-five pursuing mostly pointless endeavors. I regret the countless hours of video games that could have been spent reading and growing. I regret missed opportunities to be a good friend because I was too caught up in my own selfish priorities. I regret living without working toward my purpose or even questioning what my life meant in the grand scheme of things.

Everything we go through in life is a building block for our personal learning, but the key is using regrets and times when we are down to move forward and grow.

Over the last five years I don't have regrets. I've messed up and am far from perfect, but living intentionally had helped me to avoid disappointment over what could have been.

Is there anything in your life you fear you missed out on? You can avoid future regrets by analyzing your past and making a vow to live intentionally every single day from now on. You won't always get it right, but you'll be much better off viewing life through this lens.

Maybe you have no regrets at this time in your life. Great! Keep working at living the life you want. If you aren't moving in the right direction you are falling backwards. There is no neutral momentum, only falling backwards or making forward progress.

To avoid regret later on in life, consider tackling a new goal, doing something you've never done before, or making a plan to reinvent your lifestyle.

Lori Deschene of the popular blog Tiny Buddha, shares the following on one of her posts[9]:

> "The crazy thing about regret is that it seems imperative sometimes—as if we have to indulge it like a bed we made and now have to lie in. But there's nothing compelling us to dwell on the way things could have been. The only thing that keeps us stuck in lost possibilities is the refusal to focus on new ones."

Past regrets can motivate us to move toward bigger and brighter futures. However, we can't necessarily do everything we want to do. There are probably things in life we won't see or experience. Dwelling for too long on what might have been handicaps our future progress and will cause us to miss out on life's great opportunities.

The key is to be intentional and to be okay if you miss out on something. But make sure you are okay with missing out on it. Make the choice to skip out instead of fooling yourself into thinking it will happen later on.

One of my big hairy life goals is to write a science-fiction novel, but I haven't yet done so. This is okay with me, as I've placed other priorities and goals ahead of this dream. This means I might die having never reached this goal, and I have to be okay with that. If I'm not okay with missing out, then I need to shift priorities so I can do it right now. It's a subtle line but an important one to grasp. You need to be

---

9   Deschene, Lori. "Dealing with Regret: 8 Ways to Benefit and Move Forward." Tiny Buddha. July 10, 2017. Accessed June 08, 2019. https://tinybuddha.com/blog/dealing-with-regret-8-ways-to-benefit-and-move-forward/.

okay with missing out on some goals when the timing isn't right, but pounce when things shift.

This practical way of looking at regrets has helped to form my goals and my current priorities. If we know our top-level priorities and base decisions off of them, life gets a heck of a lot more simple and we can avoid major regret later on in life.

Question 4: What is My Number-One Goal in Life? (What's Your Destiny Goal?)

What is the main thing you are working toward right now? Do you have a major life direction and focus? If you lack direction, try crafting a mission statement for your life.

My mission statement is this: *To empower individuals to pursue their God-given potential by reducing passivity.*

I believe in a good mix of planning and action. The action piece is where a lot of people struggle. I build out all of my content with this firm goal in mind, and I enjoy talking about these topics.

This mission statement has become my number-one driving goal, and all of the other work I do should be pushing me in this direction. Even if some jobs and tasks don't directly relate, they should indirectly be serving the mission by giving me income to do the work I love, giving me more time to pursue it, or otherwise paving the way for the number-one goal to become the full-time gig.

If you don't know what your top life goal is, or feel stuck, have a brainstorming session using a Venn diagram. I know Venn diagrams might seem so fifteen minutes ago, but give it a try. It might not serve up an ace, but it could spark a future lightbulb moment.

Here's what it might look like (grab a pen and jot down your answers):

Purpose vs. Passion Venn Diagram

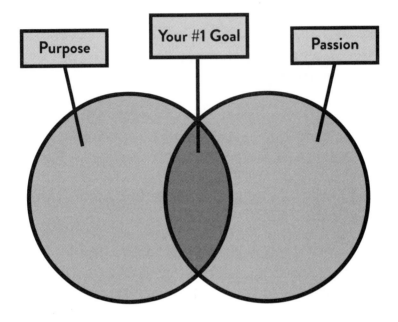

Jot down what you think your purpose in this life might be. What does the world need and what are your unique strengths? (Hint: it might help to read the whole chapter and come back). Then write down a few answers to what brings you the most joy in life. Next, in the middle of the diagram, brainstorm ways these two ideas could mix.

For example, your purpose could be to spread the love of music to the world. Your passions might consist of listening to new music or composing your own scores. Your number one goal (Destiny Goal) could be to make sure local schools expand their music curriculum.

Another trick that's useful with Venn diagrams is to write each side independent of the other. Cover up the left side as you write answers in the other. This helps to ensure you are thinking outside the box and not immediately limiting your thinking.

You can make your Venn diagram more complicated and add multiple layers, but when it comes to figuring out your number-one Destiny Goal this suffices. Remember, we are trying to answer how you are uniquely positioned to make a lasting difference in the world. There is always going to be other "stuff" we are doing. Spend time figuring out your lighthouse here.

We don't need to determine our number-one goal right this second, but take steps to figure it out. I'll reference John C. Maxwell again here:

"The two greatest days of your life are:
1)   The day you were born and;
2)   The day you find out why."

Keep working towards finding the why, and if you already know, bolster your daily habits and activities to move the needle forward.

Question 5: Will I Ever Figure Out Exactly What I am Supposed to do?

Discovering direction for your life is an ongoing process and a question you'll probably never answer fully. Even if you take the previous steps and you make Venn diagrams a daily ritual, your passion and purpose will probably change frequently and your goals will change too.

This means that five, ten, or twenty years ago your passion and life's purpose were probably not the same as today, and that's okay.

Your passion twenty-five years ago may have been woodworking for example. "Let Alex check that dining room chair, he can fix it!" But one day you might wake up and never want to see a broken wooden chair ever again.

I'm not suggesting we jump ship every time things get hard; far from it. We often have to stick with it for a while before we see meaningful results. However, many people find themselves ten years into a job they thought they might love, but are feeling like they are not fulfilling their potential to make a difference in the world. And yes, this happens to entrepreneurs too.

Do not feel stuck. You are never stuck.

We need to be constantly aware of our changing passions and the difference we are making with them in the moment. If we don't love what we are doing, no matter what it is, we should work to pull away and allow others to fill our place or be willing to shift our role.

If we are joyful givers and workers then we are impacting others at our highest potential. As entrepreneurs, this is especially relevant, because if we like what we do and it fulfills our mission statement, it's much easier to do the work and do it well, not only right now, but for the long-haul.

We will face burnout from time to time, no matter our position or love for what we do. You might be in this situation currently, which makes it even more crucial to answer these questions and take action on them one day at a time. Don't let the pain of burnout pull you away from your mission. Instead, use it to make changes and come back stronger.

Question 6: How Can I Use My Skills to Help Someone Else Right Now?

"When we are not engaged in thinking about some definite problem, we usually spend about 95 percent of our time thinking about ourselves."—Dale Carnegie, *How to Win Friends and Influence People*[10]

We spend far too much time thinking about *us*. We are conditioned to prioritize our own needs. Breaking this habit is key to long-term growth.

This question gets to the root of who you are and what you have to offer. You are an individual with a particular set of skills. Not all of us can be as awesome as Liam Neeson, but we still have special traits that no one else has.

You might think this question is impossible to answer, but not so. You know deep down what you have to offer; you just need to bring it to the light.

This question takes the focus off of us and our own selfish ambitions and instead directs our gifts, skills, passions and strengths to help other people. We need to do something that provides for our own needs and the needs of our family, but too often we miss the bigger picture.

If we shift the focus to helping others instead of lasering in on what makes us happy, we will accomplish two important goals. We will find contentment and happiness in lifting others up and helping them reach their dreams.

---

10   Carnegie, Dale. *How to Win Friends and Influence People*. Toronto: HarperCollins Canada, 2018.

For me, I don't write to become a millionaire. I write to help others and impart wisdom. With this as my focus, I can't go wrong.

We must strive to do good for others and provide value. For you, this might look like writing a book, opening a garage to help people with car repairs and maintenance, or starting a ministry to help victims of sex trafficking.

There are so many worthwhile causes out there that it might seem overwhelming to pick one. But think, if everyone did this exercise and focused their efforts on others, the world would be a much better place!

The choice comes down to what your unique skills are and what breaks your heart the most. For me, I hate seeing people stuck at a job they hate, because I was there once. I experienced the effects of what a ton of stress does to you and I'm passionate about helping others to find freedom like I did.

This passion directly feeds my ability to complete my purpose, which I believe is to help people become men and women of action. My passion is fueled by my greater purpose and it's a great place to be.

For you, it might mean starting a business or non-profit to make a difference in your local community.

If we start with this question, we will be on the right road to figuring out what the heck it is we are doing with our lives.

Question 7: Where do I Find the Time to Pursue my Passion and Discover my Purpose?

This is the ultimate question, and one I ask myself regularly. We only seem to lose time as we get older. Priorities stack up and we get more and more busy.

If we get married, our responsibilities jump. If we get a higher-paying and more demanding salaried job, our time might disappear. If we go on to have kids, then what? Sounds like we are up a creek without a paddle.

Time is the biggest reality factor we all face. We can't manufacture time out of nowhere. We all have twenty-four hours per day. Consider reducing current time wasters such as TV, free up time by finding a more flexible job, or reorganize your list of priorities.

Ideally you would find a business venture you love that pays the bills and also gives back in a meaningful way to the community. We spend most of our lives either at work or sleeping, with a small fraction of that time left over for our families and for fun activities.

As entrepreneurs, our work should be fulfilling and meaningful. If it's not, and we don't have the time to change, where did we go wrong?

Do you want to face the constant pressures of work that doesn't fulfill you? Too often we get stuck doing things the same way we've always done them and wondering why the "new freedom" of entrepreneurship isn't all it's cut out to be.

I am excited for this generation of millennial entrepreneurs who, through side hustles and personal development, answer that question with a resounding NO! No, they do not want to find themselves stuck in a job they hate with no reasonable means of escape. They would much rather work eighty hours per week on their own schedule than work forty for "the man." Sound familiar?

But with this attitude comes a tendency to overbalance and spend all of our time working with no time left for anything else. We often swing too far the other way.

Say what you want about millennials, but we are overcoming a dependence upon corporations, and as a result, greater purpose is being fulfilled.

We find ourselves in a world brimming with possibility. Some would argue we have it harder in an economy with little wiggle room for mistakes, but I disagree. I think we have immense opportunity before us, we just have to learn how to seize it, manage it, and come out stronger on the other side.

Time is born out of a willingness to reduce obligations and set priorities. There is always room for improvement and change, and the biggest factor will be getting the day job right so we can gain the level of flexibility that will meet the needs of our family and the needs of others.

Time is what we make of it. Choose to put your time towards the people, tasks, and priorities that matter most.

Question 8: What is One Small Action Step I can Take Today?

Taking positive action steps towards your next goal is the key to life change. It's the reason why I'm so obsessed with prompting people to take action. It's the best way to activate a right-now idea, learn more about yourself, and find out what you are made of.

Take the next step today to merge your passion with reality. You know what the next step is. Don't let fear stop you. Free up thirty minutes today and take the next step. Consistency is key. Thirty minutes per day adds up to fifteen hours over the course of a month. The more success you have, the more time and effort you'll want to put forth.

It's never easy to begin working towards something, especially if there are fun events happening right around you, but if you can stave off instant gratification and learn to relish the sweet taste of delayed gratification, you will find success.

Take an action step now and check one small item off your to-do list.

Question 9: What is One Thing I Could Do Every Day to Move the Needle Forward on My Big Goals?

Question nine expands on the idea of taking an action step. This question looks to a broader scheme of habit development. Instead of rushing to figure out one task for the day, be intentional about your goals and make a plan for completion.

When I go to write a book, I map out what I need to do and I set my incremental deadlines. It isn't rocket science to plan in this way, yet it works. If I schedule a due date for myself, I will get it done by the due date. If the goal has an ambiguous end date it will take much longer to achieve.

For most of us, our innate tendency is to procrastinate. Set a due date and work to get the task done by that date. The antidote to procrastination is a firm deadline. You can complete more than you give yourself credit for, so push hard. Plan out your days and see what it would take to complete the goal by breaking it down into daily activities.

For example, if you are applying to college or an advanced degree program, the goal might be to apply to one per day. If you do this over the next month, you'll have applied to thirty schools. Is this enough to meet your goal of getting in? Adjust as needed. Just a small amount of forward thinking can combat the tendency to procrastinate.

No matter what the goal is, break it down into daily tasks and then project a completion date. This is crucial for entrepreneurs so we don't get lost in the busyness and put our focus on the wrong things. Our tendency to procrastinate will die on the backs of our intentionality.

Cut yourself slack when you need it, but realize that goals won't complete themselves and big tasks can be made into much more manageable bite-sized tasks if tackled daily.

Question 10: What Will They Say in Your Eulogy?

I admit this question is a tad dark, but bear with me. Picture your funeral. You know who will step up and deliver the commentary on your life. Will the compliments be superficial, the jokes stale, and the crowd playing along but knowing the secret truth behind the well-meaning but empty praise? Or will your funeral have thousands of loving guests who travelled from near and far, trumpets blasting out Taps in honor of your legacy, and doves released in memoriam to a life well-lived?

Write out what this scene might look like if you were to die tomorrow. What would your funeral involve? Would you be proud of the way you lived your life?

Leaving a legacy means being proud of what we did with our life in terms of our impact on another life. No amount of personal accomplishment will mean anything in a few years. Trophies collect dust in attics, eventually given away for pennies in a yard sale or sneaked into a Goodwill giveaway bag. How we impact people is what keeps regrets far away and what ultimately keeps us motivated to keep going.

Don't die without giving it your best. Don't wait another second to live and work for anything less than your utmost potential.

Ponder and reflect once again on these ten important life questions:

1) What would I do if I could do anything?
2) If I could only accomplish one more thing in my life what would it be?
3) Do I have any regrets?
4) What is my number-one goal?
5) Will I ever figure out exactly what I'm supposed to do?
6) How can I use my skills to help someone else right now?
7) Where do I find the time to pursue my passion and discover my purpose?
8) What is one small action step I can take today?
9) What is one thing I can do every day to move the needle forward on my big goals?
10) What will they say in my eulogy?

Don't think for a second that it's too late to figure out your life path and direction. It doesn't matter what age you are. You're alive right now, so go out and get it done.

Answering these questions should help you think about what it is you can do with your life.

I don't know about you, but I won't wait until retirement, the kids move away, or the timing is just right in order to find a life of happiness, flexibility, and the sense that the work I do makes a difference. I will hustle now, continue to search for my passions and how I can use them to help others, and never stop growing, learning, and reflecting.

I will merge my passions with my purpose and affect positive change on this world.

I hope you will join me in doing the same. Ponder these questions often. Come back to them when you need a refresher, and always remember that each day is a new day with the opportunity to move forward.

PASSION VS. PURPOSE SELF-RATING

Are you living your passion to the fullest but still coming up empty? Are you fulfilling your purpose but missing out on the joy that life has to offer? Mark the spot where you tend to lean or check the box if you have balance in this area. We will revisit these later on so you can build your personal balance blueprint.

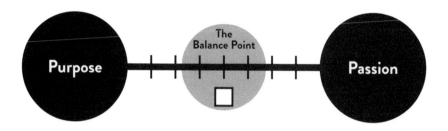

CHAPTER FIVE
REACTIVE VS. PROACTIVE

"Stamping out fires is a lot of fun, but it is only putting things back to the way they were."
—W. Edwards Deming

"We've got to be proactive. It's my job to look for unconventional situations that achieve what my clients want."
—Patrick Whitesell

Ping

Andrew and Chloe sat down at their table at La Roux Italian Restaurant.

Ping

"Andrew, didn't you say you were going to turn that off?" Chloe said with her signature smile. One that told Andrew he was good, but he might not stay that way if he didn't read between the lines.

"Ay yep. Sorry dear I forgot," said Andrew as he promptly turned his phone completely off. Tonight was about her, not work.

After a lovely evening and a few too many bites of tiramisu he returned to his home office to check for urgent work items. He had not just one, but thirty-seven new emails waiting for him. He had just spent the entire day working, minus his planned dinner with his wife. "Bugger," he thought, "I guess I won't be sleeping tonight."

And on it went like this for months. Andrew was doing his best to stay on top of email, but it seemed like every time he stepped away from his computer he'd get behind. He was finding time for his top priorities but was really struggling to manage his workload. Knowing he needed help, Andrew planned a lunch with Aaron, a good friend and fellow entrepreneur who always seemed chill, despite managing a high workload in his real estate business.

"When's the last time you looked ahead and sought problems out?" Said Aaron with a dashing smile. "We can't run our businesses like chickens with our heads cut off. We have to look ahead and learn how to anticipate setbacks and potential issues."

Andrew liked Aaron, but right now he wanted to smack the grin off his friend's face. He was putting in a ton of time and didn't like being compared to a headless chicken. But yet… The words rang true. He stared at his friend with a smile forming behind disbelieving eyes.

"Okay, that all sounds nice, but how?" Andrew said.

Aaron shoveled down a bite of pork bbq and continued, "You've got to look ahead and seek out issues. This has kept me sane through some crazy busy times. I know it's the last thing you want to do but trust me, invest time thinking in advance and your life will be so much easier."

Andrew looked at Aaron suspiciously, "Okay… I'll give it a try, but I don't really believe you. Does this really work?" He had so much going on and so much to deal with, he couldn't picture himself taking steps to look ahead, he was just barely keeping his head above water.

"Haha dude this really works. Not right away, mind you, but just try it and let me know how it goes."

Andrew went back home that night and took Aaron's advice. He jotted down what he thought were potential issues, questions, and needs that might arise in his business.

Over the coming weeks he took action and sought out potential issues. He was learning to be more intentional by checking in with clients regularly, taking note of ways he could go above and beyond, and becoming more organized. Then, the magic began. His inbox became manageable, his business was thriving, and he felt more balanced than ever before.

He looked out his office window and muttered "Okay Aaron, I guess you were right this time…" And so Andrew sent a thank you card Aaron's way, remembering his time with Doris and wanting to emulate gratitude by showing how thankful he was.

- -

Finding the balance point between putting out the fires burning right now, and looking for problems is tricky. Learning to be reactive during times of intense heat and also finding the time, no matter what, to plan and look ahead is challenging.

We all have a sense of reactiveness ingrained within us. It's easy to respond to email inquiries with relatively little planning ahead. It's simple to sit and wait for the phone to ring. Dealing with known problems is child's play compared to seeking out issues and watering down the ember before it becomes a full-blown forest fire.

Putting out future fires is about having a mindset wherein you see past the current wildfires and don't get distracted by the noise of everyday business. It's about putting yourself in the shoes of customers, business partners, and associates and asking what could happen. What might derail the customer experience? What issue might the interns have today (again)? What will my associates, coworkers, or fellow entrepreneurs need from me today that will be easier to deal with in advance?

Current problems tend to drown out your time to look ahead. You must be intentional to avoid spending too much time on the most urgent issues.

Oftentimes it can seem like we are swimming in a sea of problems. The neat thing about problems is that at some point you will start to see patterns. If you are running a startup this might not be true right away, but eventually you'll realize Annie from accounting has the same problems every Friday afternoon when payroll is due and she can't figure out how to work Gusto.

You know your team and your environment better than you think. What problems can you foresee? What can you do about the problems now before the fire gets too big to manage? Better yet, what problems have occurred before that might happen again?

Once you start to think in this way, there is a danger of seeing everything as a problem, so with every piece of advice in this book be sure that you don't swing too far in the other direction. You don't want to start seeing problems that don't really exist, or forget to deal with the urgent issues your team is facing today.

A good entrepreneur works to solve current problems that require a good reactive manager. A next-level entrepreneur knows how to address the problem before it exists.

Seven Elements to a Balanced Approach to Work Problems:

1) Take initiative: When you see an issue developing, jump on it and tackle it before it gets out of hand.

2) Trust your intuition: Learn to trust your gut.

3) Look for patterns: What might come up in the future that will take time away from you and your team? What are the patterns

you are beginning to see? What issues repeat themselves and have no clear solution?

4) Tackle big problems first: Deal with the big fires in the moment and be reactive when necessary. Don't let the fires smolder.

5) Do a post-problem assessment: What went wrong here? Don't assign blame, but work together as a team to ensure the problem is avoided or mitigated in the future.

6) Plan: Ensure a plan is put in place derived from the post-problem assessment.

7) Take action: Don't sit idle. As an entrepreneur, it's on you to call for movement towards a better work environment for all. Taking swift and determined action is your ticket to finding balance with problems in the workplace.

1) Initiative

Initiative is the flint to the steel of fire setting. Set the right fires and blaze your own path. Strong initiative isn't easy in a hectic and problematic environment, but you'll need to start somewhere.

Entrepreneurs with high levels of initiative:

- Never ask, "What should I be doing today?"
- Always do more than is expected of them. Yes, this means doing more than you expect of yourself.
- Run their team with progress in mind instead of maintaining the status quo.
- Say what needs to be said, when it needs to be said. They aren't afraid of difficult conversations if having them will move the company forward.
- Act confidently and with humility.

- Ask for feedback and actively listen to others.

- Prepare for the worst but expect the best.

- Never stop asking questions of themselves, their employees, and business associates.

Learn to take the initiative in order to become more proactive in your everyday work environment. Tackle the challenge head on and you'll quickly find that you'll get more done than ever before.

Get on the ball and start setting your own positive fires in your workplace and life.

2) Trust Your Intuition

Intuition is a muscle that must be exercised. Our gut reaction is right more often than not, according to Malcolm Gladwell in his book *Blink*.[11] He says, "Decisions made very quickly can be every bit as good as decisions made cautiously and deliberately."

Blink is a fascinating book and I recommend giving it a read. It highlights why our intuition is a force to be reckoned with. Trusting our "gut feeling" isn't always the right course, but it can lead us in more good directions than bad if we learn how to listen to it and then act on it. The power of the subconscious at making quick and accurate decisions is something every entrepreneur should consider tapping into.

One way to practice intuition is to put aside reason and logic for a minute. Simply ask yourself how the person or situation is making you feel, and why.

Our intuitive sense is based off our own experiences. Look at

---

11   Gladwell, Malcolm. *Blink: The Power of Thinking Without Thinking*. New York: Back Bay Books, 2013.

beginner's luck. You've no doubt heard of it or even experienced it for yourself. I have. The first time I ever fired a shotgun was with two close friends. We were out to shoot clay pigeons. I'd never held a real gun before, so naturally I had no clue what I was doing. My friend's dad was a game warden, and he had been a hunter all of his life. He was a natural and really good at explaining how to shoot. He was also really good at shooting clay pigeons and hit nineteen out of twenty-five.

My stats for the day? I hit twenty-four out of twenty-five.

Trust your gut and channel your intuitive leanings into making the best decisions for your business.

3) Tackle Big Problems First

Big problems are where you naturally channel your reactive tendencies. Identify what problems are at the forefront right now, and handle them accordingly. Tackle the obvious blazing flames first.

As you calm the fires and embrace the importance of being proactive, don't forget the skills you need to react quickly to problems. Big problems that come to the door while you are working a long-term plan might need to be dealt with. Don't ignore the massive blazes even if you are finding success with foresight.

You might find yourself in a place of complete chaos, unable to make it through even the smallest of fires. That's okay. Those times occur. In order to find balance, you will need to move on from the daily problems that come to the forefront and look at the root causes. If your daily work life is in complete chaos there is likely an underlying reason why.

4) Look for Problems

Problems in business are commonplace. The longer you are in your field, the more you'll be able to predict issues before they arise. Embrace this learning and use it to move a step further.

Looking for problems means asking tough questions:

- What can we be doing better?
- Are we holding team members accountable?
- Do we have clear goals, and does the entire team know and share these goals?
- What problems keep recurring?
- What is the one problem I hate thinking about (and wish would just go away)?

Bring these types of problems to the forefront and get ready to tackle them. Bring in help when needed, but don't avoid problems that won't go away. The fire will only burn brighter over time.

5) Do a Post-Problem Assessment

Once you tackle and snuff out a problem, the easiest thing you can do is to shake hands with everyone around the table, go out for drinks at the end of the day, and forget the issue ever occurred.

Don't make this mistake. The problem will almost always come back and rear its ugly head. If it happened once, it will probably happen again.

For example, let's say your biggest customer never received an order they placed two weeks ago. They reached out and wondered what was causing the delay. You checked into it and found out it was never processed. Whoops.

Learn to handle a big problem with reactive grace, and then use the problem to instill proactive chutzpah into your team as well. Don't let a mistake like the previous example happen a second time or you might lose business.

Set up a time to check in and discuss what happened. Don't assign blame but work to determine where the breakdown occurred. Rehashing will be painful; remember, the hope is to avoid spending time and resources on the same problem later on. The truth is that calling something what it is and recognizing the problem is almost always better than ignoring it and hoping it fixes itself. It won't.

While you rehash what happened, take notes on how you solved the issue. This will give you insight into why the problem occurred, and whether the fix is temporary or permanent.

Now that you've replayed the footage, you can move forward with an intentional eye.

6) Make a Plan

Singapore is one of the most beautifully clean and organized places on Earth. It's a country and also a city, but it doesn't have the normal grimy city vibes that are par for the course in most US cities.

My wife and I took a trip there recently and were blown away by rows and rows of tall trees dotting the highways, lush parks and greenways, and a subway system so clean you could eat a pie off the floor and not get sick.

It wasn't always this way.

On October 1st 1968, Prime Minister Lee Kuan Yew launched the "Keep Singapore Clean Campaign." Prime Minister Yew saw a growing problem of litter, dirt, and general filth throughout the city.

His vision for a beautiful Singapore was not playing out in the real world and he saw it as a major problem.

In launching the campaign, Yew made an intentional plan to make the city clean. He went all in, enforcing heavy fines for littering, organizing city-wide clean-up days, and urging citizens to plant trees. He instilled a sense of pride in his people that carries on to this day. Even foreigners know that to litter or chew gum risks offending the country's citizens or incurring heavy fines. Current-day Singapore is one of the cleanest places you will ever visit. It's a true testament to what intentional planning, foresight, and decisive action can do.

Using the notes from the assessment stage, make a plan of action for the next time a problem occurs. Put steps in place to avoid the problem altogether.

You can implement a formal plan if you'd like, or make the plan of action more fun and memorable. You could even hold an event named after the problem, like "Jerry's Big Screwup, Let's not be Jerry" or something equally ridiculous and memorable. (Make sure Jerry is okay with an evening in his honor first.) A memorable moment like this will serve to remind everyone involved that you'd rather not have deja vu with another "Jerry."

You just went through hell and back with the latest issue in your business; the least you can do is to take advantage of the successful outcome by making a solid plan to address the issue in the future.

The point is to use failure and setback as a stepping point for future success.

7) Take action

Once you have a plan in place, don't be surprised when things fall apart again. It will happen. Do the best you can to stay balanced between reaction and proaction. Keep an eye out for future issues, but don't forget to tackle major issues on your doorstep as they arise.

Taking decisive action is what moves us forward as entrepreneurs. No matter what level of business you've achieved, finding a sense of balance between reactive and proactive measures is of paramount importance to business success. No matter what skills you need to employ next, take intentional action to overcome adversity.

Even if there are just two people on your team, or if you work by yourself, do these same exercises. Don't forget, it's important to assess and figure out what went wrong in order to avoid dealing with the same issues over and over. Don't let your dream die because of recurring problems.

REACTIVE VS. PROACTIVE SELF-RATING

Do you tend to respond to crises as they come or do you spend too much time thinking about what might happen? Mark the spot where you tend to lean or check the box if you have balance in this area. We will revisit these later on so you can build your personal balance blueprint.

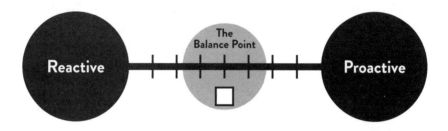

CHAPTER SIX

INTENTION VS. PERCEPTION

"A gift consists not in what is done or given, but in the intention of the giver or doer.
—Lucius Annaeus Seneca

"The most important thing in communication is hearing what isn't said."
—Peter Drucker

Andrew walked in the door of his modest home in the heart of Chicago, feeling happy after a long run. But as soon as he stepped inside he could sense something was off.

Chloe was sitting in the living room with her legs crossed. She issued a loud "harrumph" as Andrew walked into her line of sight.

"Andrew, you still haven't fixed the sink. I wish you would do the things you say you'll do," Chloe said quickly, as if she was immediately regretting it.

Andrew became immediately defensive, "What are you talking about? I've only had the new garbage disposal for a few days."

"It's been on the table for three weeks now," Chloe said with a rising voice. "I've had to eat all my meals in the living room, and I'm getting sick of not having the table to do my scrapbooking." Chloe stood up like a bear protecting her young, a fierce stance that had Andrew on the defensive.

"You haven't scrapbooked in over three years," Andrew said with a biting tone. He could feel his blood rising. He hated fighting, but he

THE BALANCE POINT

didn't like being chastised. He was a busy guy and didn't have time to fix the sink right now.

Their argument continued for several hot minutes and ended when Chloe walked over and slammed the bedroom door yelling "enjoy sleeping on the couch tonight, blankets are in the den." And with that she quickly opened up the door once more, tossed out his pillow, and clicked the lock.

Andrew jumped in the shower in a rage, unable to settle down. He had no idea this was such a big deal to Chloe.

He jumped out of the shower still fuming, got dressed, walked downstairs, and turned on the TV. As he sat there still upset he remembered the feelings of helping his neighbor Doris. It had made him truly happy to assist her with her TV. Shouldn't he want to do even more for his wife?

Feeling guilty and wanting to do something about it he decided to jump in now and see what he could do. He set an away message on his email, shut his computer down, and funneled his anger into the project.

Several hours later Chloe walked out of the bedroom. "What the heck are you doing Andrew? It's 3 AM!" she said with a shriek, but with a smile secretly displayed on her face.

Andrew looked up, pulled his safety glasses down slightly, and said with still a bit of anger behind his voice. "I'm fixing the sink. I'm still pretty mad though, you know I hate sleeping on the couch. You also realize I'm not the handy one right? I looked all over for the Philips screwdriver and we don't have one."

"I know," she said, "I'm sorry for overreacting. Are you really fixing it right now? You don't have to do that. Here, let me help."

"Please do," he said.

Now laughing Chloe said, "You always were pretty bad with tools." She found the Phillips immediately and walked over to help him undo his many mistakes.

As they worked, the anger of their argument fell away.

Andrew looked over at Chloe and said, "You could have said something. I've been so busy I didn't even think about putting the disposal in. I was going to do it when I got around to it." As he said this he got up and embraced his wife with a fervent hug. "I'm sorry again, love. I wasn't thinking. I never want you to think I don't care."

"I know you care, it just seemed like you didn't really want to finish this. You're the one who told me you'd do it saying you 'wanted to be the man and fix something.' I wouldn't care so much had you not promised. You know I could have done this on my own. Next time I'll tell you how I feel early on so you don't have to work through the night like a crazy person. Come to bed. You can finish this on the weekend. I'll cancel our plans to see my mom."

"That might be the best news I've ever heard," Andrew said as he started laughing.

Chloe smacked him on the back of the head hard enough to hurt, but light enough to be playful.

They both went to bed happy things had worked out. They weren't sure where they'd be cooking for the next couple days as Andrew had blown a circuit in the kitchen, but at least for now they were on the same team.

- -

Communication rests on the shoulders of your intentions for an outcome, mixed with the other person's perception of your intention.

If you say one thing, and mean it 100%, it doesn't mean that the other person understood or even cares about your intentions. What they perceive is what matters to them, and you'd be wise to care about that. Even if you have the best of intentions for another person, it might not matter if they don't see where you are coming from.

Communication is essential to any business and entrepreneurial venture. We must be able to communicate effectively to build solid relationships with clients, business partners, and other like-minded entrepreneurs.

What we say matters.

What we mean matters.

What the other person understands and interprets matters, too.

Think about this scenario. You are a highly successful venture capital business that has just outgrown its office space due to a high volume of new clients. As the owner and CEO you decide to build a brand new building in the heart of a bustling city district complete with high ceilings, a pretty view of the city, and a top-of-the-line espresso machine. You think your employees will find the new space comforting and fun to work in, and your clients will appreciate and respect your upgrades.

False.

What actually happens is your employees hate the new commute and your clients think they are now paying for the luxury space with their increased monthly dues.

You thought they would love the new office and perks, but your intentions for increasing your company's perceived value backfired. Your clients just want incredible results and your employees want to be paid well at a job with a short commute.

Consider the importance of making your intentions known in order to invite feedback on how your intentions are perceived from another point of view.

I didn't understand why perception mattered so much until working with one of my managers at the retirement community where my wife and I spent several years.

Betty had good intentions. I believe she cared about the residents. But several residents of the community complained that she was extremely rude. Betty was rude to residents, employees, and visitors on more than one occasion. Because we knew her well, we realized that she truly did care, but she was stressed and had a hard time staying patient enough to show it.

This taught me a valuable lesson: Regardless of how much we care, if we don't show it the right way, how are other people supposed to know?

Theodore Roosevelt said, "Nobody cares how much you know until they know how much you care." Care enough to ask the right questions and be self-aware enough to gauge how you are coming across.

We would do well to have positive and affirming intentions to do right by others. If we don't, even positive perceptions from others are based on lies.

At the same time, having the right intentions and following through on those intentions by creating the reality for others is key, and something to strive for.

Here are five quick ways to find a balance between intention and perception:

1) Enhance your empathy muscle.

2) Manage your intentions.

3) Ask for feedback and be willing to accept criticism.

4) Don't blame others for how they feel.

5) Take one step forward.

1) Enhance your Empathy Muscle

To master the art of managing intentions and perceptions, we must learn to understand and empathize with people.

There are whole books written on empathy. To put it simplistically, empathy is noticing the feelings of others. Focus on what people actually mean instead of what they are saying. Don't take their words at face value; dig deeper.

Active, empathetic listening involves caring enough about what the other person says to understand where they are coming from.

People with high levels of empathy are good at understanding and experiencing the feelings of others. Sympathetic people actively care about how the person feels and want to do whatever possible to help them.

To increase your empathy muscle:

- Put yourself in your client's or employee's shoes. What would it be like to work with you? I wouldn't like working with me sometimes, and I also wouldn't hire myself for certain tasks. Keep this in mind when improving empathy.

- Ask open-ended questions to get to know people on a deeper level. Let them do the talking and listen to their answers.

- Be curious why people think the way they do. Few people are "crazy," they just think differently than you. Seek to understand why they disagree with your perspective.

- Initiate healthy discussion. Steer clear of rants on social media. Instead, lead a local book club and ask thought provoking questions.

In business and in life, we can't realistically help everyone, so empathy is the desired path here. We need to feel out how folks react to what we say and do, even if there may not be time to handle each issue and person specifically and have sympathy towards everyone.

Learn how to experience the feelings of others, and if you can't reliably do so, bring someone into the fold who can help relay this information to you. This in turn will help you to learn empathy, which is a powerful skill for all entrepreneurs to learn.

2) Manage your Intentions.

If you want to fire your VA or assistant every time they make a mistake, why is that? Do you have the best of intentions for him or her?

Intentions are often hidden from others. What's even more dangerous is hiding them from ourselves.

Take a long, hard look at your own selfish tendencies. If we don't truly want the best for others, why is that? If an employee needs to be let go that's one thing, but having the best of intentions for a successful working relationship is a good place to start. Manage your intentions and do your best to strive for the success of others.

Some clients will be great and some will be difficult. Some projects will suck the life out of you and others will give you limitless energy. Some employees are more effort than they're worth and some will make your life so much easier. Make sure that for either type you are valuing the person and truly want the best for them. Having a love of people will go a long way towards managing your intentions.

3) Ask for Feedback and be Willing to Accept Criticism

Asking questions and starting a dialogue is the easiest way to feel out how people perceive your intentions. This is the key to bridging the gap between intentions and real-life perceptions.

This is especially hard when you have the best of intentions for the people you work with. Come to grips with the fact that everyone sees things differently. You don't have to be perfect and adjust course for every person, but knowing the general vibe others get from you is super important for self-growth and increasing business viability.

Don't be afraid to accept the feedback and then act on what you know to be true. If others' perceptions of you are not meeting your intentions, then you might be doing something wrong.

Experiment with small changes at first and see how others react. Maybe all you need to do is check in with certain people once per day and ask them how they are doing. Personal interaction can go a long way in filling the intention-perception gap.

Be a leader and entrepreneur who relishes the challenge of being pliable and working to change and grow. Embrace humility and realize you have a long way to go. People will respect you for your willingness to change and grow.

4) Let Others Feel How They Feel

Some people are never going to be happy. There are some folks who won't ever believe your positive intentions, even if you go out of your way each day to prove you care.

Don't get stuck on these folks, and don't blame them for how they feel. Sometimes the healthiest solution is to move on and part ways. Some people just don't vibe with others and that's okay. Don't take it on yourself to fix every problem and to be liked by everyone; that is NOT what this chapter is about.

Do your best to manage your intentions. Figure out how team members are really doing, but don't exhaust yourself with Bob when he doesn't even really want to be on the team anyway.

5) Take One Step Forward with One Person

Take steps to ensure that your intentions are playing out in reality.

Miscommunications occur at many levels, and communication itself is a topic far beyond the scope of this book.

Suffice it to say that the more you can learn about how to communicate effectively with others, the better and smoother your operation will run.

Pick out one person in your life to focus on. Ask that person to coffee or invite them on a Zoom call. Figure out what their wants and needs are. Make a plan of action to encourage them, but also to find out if you are being perceived as you think you are. Ask them for candid thoughts on how you run your business or even your ability to be a good friend to them. Don't take this person's word as law, but use it to formulate new thoughts on the real-life implications of how you are being perceived.

Beyond this personal interaction, set clear expectations and guidelines for your business. Let others know exactly what a good result looks like, and do your best to cultivate an atmosphere that invites feedback. Ask questions of yourself and others to keep an open line of communication, and your ability to strike the perfect balance between your positive intentions, and others' feelings towards your actions, will increase.

Remember the importance of this avenue, and you will move further along the path to becoming a balanced entrepreneur.

INTENTION VS. PERCEPTION SELF-RATING

What's more important to you, intention or perception? Do you hope people are reading your intentions without worrying about how they perceive your actions? Or maybe you have the best of intentions but just aren't sure how to communicate your actions. Mark the spot where you tend to lean or check the box if you have balance in this area. We will revisit these later on so you can build your personal balance blueprint.

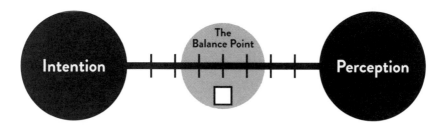

CHAPTER SEVEN
CONSUMPTION VS. PRODUCTION

"Books are the quietest and most constant of friends; they are the most accessible and wisest of counselors, and the most patient of teachers."
—Charles W. Eliot

"Productivity is never an accident. It is always the result of a commitment to excellence, intelligent planning, and focused effort."
—Paul J. Meyer

Andrew hit publish on his most recent blog post. It lacked his usual gusto and flair, and he could feel the energy drain from his soul even thinking about reading it over again. It was bad.

Working from his newly renovated kitchen, Andrew slumped over his laptop. With Chloe's supervision, he had spent the last several weeks replacing not only the garbage disposal, but the fridge, countertops, and cabinetry. He was exhausted, but knew Chloe appreciated his efforts. Now he had to shift gears and get back to writing.

His audience expected him to post something new each day, and he had to stick to his schedule. He owed it to his following to keep great content coming, but it was becoming increasingly difficult to be creative.

The next day, he did nothing at all. He couldn't bring himself to write no matter how hard he tried. And then a week went by and people were pestering him on social media to see if he was all right. He would send a quick thumbs up and get back to the blank page, willing his fingers to move and his mind to create. Nothing.

"I'm stuck, Chlo'," Andrew proclaimed one night over dinner.

"With...?" said Chloe, without looking up from her soup.

"I don't have a single good idea left to write about. I'm tapped out."

"Well, what have you been reading lately? Oh yeah, not much huh?" Chloe said with a wink; they'd had this discussion many times.

"If I've learned nothing else the past few years, it's that I probably should listen to my wife," Andrew said with a resigned sigh.

"You got that right big guy."

"Don't let it go to your head, hun," Andrew said as he started browsing his phone's library app for books that would pique his interest.

A few minutes later Andrew said excitedly, "Chloe, I just borrowed a bunch of books. I can't wait to read them all."

"But Andrew you haven't read a book in over a year..." Chloe said with a little sigh.

"Don't worry, dear. I made a goal. I got this. Want to join me? This was your idea after all."

"Oh goodness what have I done..." Chloe muttered under her breath. "Okay I'll do it, but I'm not just reading presidential biographies. We've gotta throw some fun stuff in there too."

"That's not a problem. Let's do this."

"Oh and by the way," said Chloe, "you should read this book I just started called *What to Expect When You're Expecting*."

Dumbfounded, Andrew did nothing except stare at his wife in shock.

When he got over the initial confusion he scooped Chloe up in a warm embrace and held her close for several minutes.

Andrew spent the next few months devouring books and doing the best he could to keep up with his commitments. He read on breaks, he read during lunch, and he amazed his online community when he missed three episodes of *Game of Thrones* because he "had to finish reading the book on being a great dad."

After finishing only a few new books he could feel his mind opening up. He sat down at the computer and bam! New ideas flew from his brain.

It made perfect sense, but it also seemed counterintuitive that reading would help him create content. Reading was his newfound superpower and he would use it for good.

- -

Learning and creating are a key balance point for all entrepreneurs. When we start on the journey we consume everything we can on a topic, sometimes leading to analysis paralysis. This new knowledge leads to a burst of creative energy, until that dries up, and you find yourself uninspired and drained from all the energy you expended with nothing new to draw from. Put simply, mastering consumption vs. production relies on a balanced give and take of the two forces.

On the one hand you have content consumption and learning. On the other hand you have the production and creation of new content. We have to merge these two forces and be good at both in order to be in our businesses for the long haul and continue to produce content we can be proud of.

Reading books is the area I am going to focus on as it's usually where entrepreneurs struggle. It fits into our routines to search for short blogs or videos to answer our pressing questions, whereas reading books takes an intentional effort.

Reading is one of the most powerful ways to grow your mind and increase your capacity to create. We can learn how to do things via a quick video, but diving deeper is what causes our brains to engage, and this deep engagement in turn sparks new creativity. We don't know what we don't know, and reading books often gives us answers to questions we didn't know we needed to ask.

We don't really need to be told how to do something, after all; what we need is to learn it ourselves. We need to learn how to think like an expert and train our minds to figure it out on our own next time.

Reading is a superpower we all have access to. A 2013 study[12] that appeared in *Neurology Journal* found that reading books can help to keep memory and thinking skills intact. The Wall Street Journal shares that reading can help fend off depression and anxiety,[13] and a study released in *Neurology* showed that reading could slow the cognitive decline of dementia.[14]

---

12   Wilson, Robert S., Patricia A. Boyle, Lei Yu, Lisa L. Barnes, Julie A. Schneider, and David A. Bennett. "Life-span Cognitive Activity, Neuropathologic Burden, and Cognitive Aging." Neurology. July 23, 2013. Accessed June 08, 2019. http://www.neurology.org/content/81/4/314.abst ract.

13   Helliker, Kevin. "Bibliotherapy: Reading Your Way To Mental Health." The Wall Street Journal. August 01, 2007. Accessed June 08, 2019. https://www.wsj .com/articles/SB118583572352482728.

14   Wilson, Robert S., Patricia A. Boyle, Lei Yu, Lisa L. Barnes, Julie A. Schneider, and David A. Bennett. "Life-span Cognitive Activity, Neuropathologic Burden, and Cognitive Aging." Neurology. July 23, 2013. Accessed June 08, 2019. https://n.neurology.org/content/81/4/314.

Need one more rock-solid reason to read? Reading has also been shown to give us an increased tolerance for uncertainty.[15] Since we, as entrepreneurs, live in uncertainty day to day, I say with conviction that every one of us should be reading more.

Let's talk about how we can do more of it and become even more successful as entrepreneurs.

How to Read More as an Entrepreneur

The best way to do something (and then do more of something) is to be first convinced that it's important (I hope I've done that for you) and then come up with a way to follow through. Here are six quick ways entrepreneurs can read more without investing more than a few hours per week:

1) Find Ways to Add Reading to Tasks You Are Already Doing

One easy way to read more is by listening to audiobooks. You can use your local library's audio services or sign up for a service like Audible and get brand-new, best-selling books each month.

Listening to audiobooks allows you to read while you drive, cook, or complete mindless work tasks that don't require your full focus.

2) Read for Fun

One simple way to read more is to find fiction books that you love. Sure, it's not going to give you unique business strategies or top-notch ideas to increase productivity, but reading in any capacity is still helpful for your mind and much better than watching TV. (Sidenote:

---

15   Jacobs, Tom. "Study: Reading Novels Makes Us Better Thinkers." Salon. June 15, 2013. Accessed June 08, 2019. https://www.salon.com/2013/06/15/book_nerds_make_better_decisions_partner/.

most ways we entertain ourselves are better than TV, including video games, since we are at least using our minds to complete tasks or talk to other gamers online.)

If you usually read non-fiction, try a new fiction genre every once in a while to keep your reading fresh. You might find mystery novels intrigue you, or that vampire romances keep you turning pages late into the night.

Since any book counts as expanding your mind and increasing your ability to create new ideas, branch out and find books you love to read. If you do so, it won't be hard to develop (or reacquire) a love of reading.

3) Read for 30 Minutes a Day

The easiest way to develop a habit is to be consistent and do the habit daily. Do you have room in your schedule for thirty minutes of reading every day? Most of us do.

I have a daily auto reminder that comes up on my Trello board that prompts me to read for thirty minutes before I get into anything else. It has helped me to remember to read often.

I still don't read every day. Sometimes I silence the reminder and go on to "more important things." I do find that my work ethic and determination is increased when I read daily, and it's a habit I want to cultivate and keep working on.

Reading every single day, even if it's just for a few minutes, is a great way to create a love of reading.

4) Set a Reading Goal

One of the best ways to accomplish anything is to set a goal. As an entrepreneur you know this. Apply it to reading too.

Set a goal to read a certain number of books in the coming year. Last year I set a goal to read fifty books for the year. I ended up crushing the goal and read around seventy. I never would have read even close to this amount had I not made it a major priority and given myself a big goal to hit.

Just like we need to set achievement goals and deadlines for our businesses and online endeavors, we need to remember the importance of setting goals beyond vague ideas such as "I'd like to read more." Be specific and have a destination in mind. Do it for your personal growth. Pick a number of books that will stretch you and force you to read, but isn't so high you give up right away.

5) Read all Different Book Formats And Keep a Book on You at All Times

I always have an audiobook, Kindle, and a paperback going at the same time. This allows me to read without the glare of a screen, when I'm in line at Starbucks, or while I'm walking, driving, or cooking.

Keep a book on you at all times and you'll always have the opportunity to use your time to read, instead of playing your favorite game on your phone. Don't get distracted by pointless time wasters; choose to read instead.

6) Be Proactive and Not Reactive with Your Reading

As we discussed in a previous chapter, the benefits of being proactive can be applied to reading too. Instead of only reading things that pop up on your computer or emails that come in, schedule time to read.

There are some books that will be impactful on your life, but if you don't plan to read you might never read them.

If you've never read *How to Win Friends and Influence People,* you ought to, and if you haven't, why not? You've probably heard of this groundbreaking and timeless book on cultivating personal relationships, and you know relationships are huge for business growth, but maybe you haven't run into the need to read a book that shows you how to get better in this realm. Sometimes we know we need something, but unless we have a compelling reason to do it in the moment, we miss out on potential growth opportunities.

When you are intentional about your reading, you read great books that are guaranteed to have a positive impact on your life, your business, and your relationships.

Three Strategies to Avoid Analysis by Paralysis and Content Overconsumption

Reading is vital for growth, but we have to do our due diligence and recognize that too much of a good thing can be a bad thing.

If we read too much, we can get locked into a sense of analysis paralysis. This is never good for growth. Learning how to avoid this trap is the key to balance in the content consumption and production realm.

Here are three strategies for a balanced approach to excellent productivity:

1) Strategy #1: Gain one important concept from each book you read

2) Strategy #2: Take action often

3) Strategy #3: Be clear about your goal

Mastering these strategies will help you if you tend to fall on the spectrum of either reading too much or spending too much time trying to figure it all out on paper instead of acting on it in the real world.

Strategy #1: Gain One Important Concept From Each Book You Read

One way to ensure that you don't get bogged down in consuming too much content is by making a habit to pull out one new idea, strategy, or concept from everything you read.

It doesn't have to be earth shattering. As you read each book, determine the most important theme the author is trying to convey and write it down in your journal. Do this for fiction and non-fiction. Every book has a lesson, even if it's hidden deep within the pages. Start to think of the major themes from the book and ask yourself what they mean for you and how you can apply them.

For example, in this book I hope to stress the importance of mastering the yin and yang of life and to assure you that you can find a balance. You might get something entirely different out of the book and that's great. What you learn from it and apply to your life might be entirely different than what the author intended, but remember one important takeaway and if you can, apply it to your life.

Strategy #2: Take Action Often

The key to a good sense of balance between consumption and creation is to take action often. This means reading and writing. It means watching a YouTube video or Udemy course of how to do something and then going off and actually doing it. It means asking yourself what you could be doing better and making it a point to do that one thing.

Taking action is simple, and yet it's the most effective way of learning how to do something. Don't be afraid of failure. Do.

If you read the aforementioned book *How to Win Friends and Influence People*, you'll recognize the importance of giving people the opportunity to save face in a conversation or situation even if they are dead wrong. Recognizing this, and actually doing it out in the real world are two very different things. Taking a chance and putting the advice into action is how we truly remember what we've learned.

Just recently, I read a fascinating book called *Never Split the Difference*[16] by Chris Voss. In it, the author tells the story of his years of working as a hostage negotiator with the FBI. Among other tips and strategies for communication, Voss shares how open-ended questions are one easy way to drive conversation and, ultimately, get what we want.

After reading, I decided to quickly take action and try it out in the real world. I went downstairs to the barista in the coffee shop where I was typing away on this book. Instead of asking "how much for a refill on my iced coffee?" I said "how would I go about getting a refill for my coffee?" A subtle difference, but open ended. I was asking the barista to help me with my problem instead of directly asking for a refill.

The barista smiled and said "Oh that's no problem give me a sec," and returned shortly after with a fresh cup of deliciously smooth (and free!) iced coffee.

Would this have happened if I had asked how much? Maybe. Maybe not. The point is this lesson is now stuck in my brain since I actually put it into practice. Read all the books you want, but unless we start

---

16   Voss, Christopher A., and Tahl Raz. *Never Split the Difference: Negotiating as If Your Life Depended on It*. London: Rh Business Books, 2017.

to take action and implement the learned strategies into our lives, we won't see long-term success.

Strategy #3: Be Clear About Your Goals

If you know where you want to go, it's easier to get there. It's also easier to know when you've arrived. When it comes to handling decisions and knowing which choices are best, compare your thoughts on the subject with the clear goals you've set for your company or business.

If the goal is going to help move the needle forward, work toward the goal. If the goal or tasks don't relate or you don't think they will help, pass.

I believe that we often know what the right direction is, but we are often fearful of the outcome of taking a new direction. This causes us to overthink, overanalyze, and go into a panic mode. But if you're clear on your goals and what you want your outcomes to be, more often than not you'll avoid failure.

Not being able to make a decision only gets worse in proportion to the impact of the decision. If you can't decide what to get for dinner your kids might go crazy but they won't starve. If you are unsure of whether to take the new job offer, more is riding on the decision. But not making a decision is making a choice too. Take the time you need for big decisions, but don't overanalyze.

Practice and strengthen your decision-making muscle often and work hard to develop a system of counterbalances you trust.

At the end of the day, few decisions are unfixable. Do your due diligence to craft a strong mind and a base of productive habits. Consume, act, consume, act again, and don't get bottled up on either side.

CONSUMPTION VS. PRODUCTION SELF-RATING

Do you read or view educational content in your niche so much that your eyes hurt? Do you tend to work so hard and so often you don't have time for new learning? Mark the spot where you tend to lean or check the box if you have balance in this area. We will revisit these later on so you can build your personal balance blueprint.

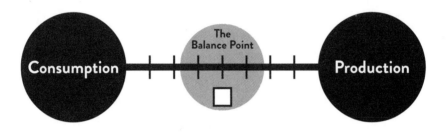

CHAPTER EIGHT

INSTANT WIN VS. DELAYED GRATIFICATION

"Live life for the moment because everything else is uncertain!"
—Louis Tomlinson

"If you will live like no one else, later you can live like no one else."
—Dave Ramsey

"I love it, let's buy it!" Chloe shrieked with glee as she stared longingly at the house by the lake.

"I really like it too, but it's a bit outside of our price range." Andrew couldn't hide a hint of disappointment in his tone. He stepped into their car, ready to leave the gorgeous lake house.

"We have to make this place work. It's gorgeous, and it has just the right amount of space for our growing family." As she said this Chloe patted her stomach and smiled down at it.

"I know love, I agree," Andrew said. He reached over and put his hand on her hand resting comfortably on her baby bump. "We are gonna need all the space we can get."

Later that night Andrew called his realtor. "We'll take it." He'd have to cash out some investments, but he would make it work. The house would be perfect for his growing family and worth every penny.

One week later...

He read the note again. This time he didn't even marvel at the irony that it had been written on yellow parchment paper obviously pulled out of a legal pad. He angrily pulled at the edges as he read:

Dear Andrew,

Thank you for your time with us these last seven years. The board has appreciated your time and energy working to secure a long-term future in this ever-changing atmosphere.

We regret to inform you that this letter serves as your termination effective immediately. It has come to our attention that you cashed out one of our largest assets and deposited the money into your account. As this is your right to do so as the CEO, we are not inclined to pursue legal action against you, but the viability of this company has been threatened by your actions.

Thereby, we will not stand idly by and watch as this company starts a downward spiral. We have voted unanimously that new leadership be sought and a new structure built. We owe it to ourselves and our partners to move forward in a direction that is best for all.

We wish you the best of luck in your future endeavors.

-The board

"It's not every day you get thrown out of your own company," thought Andrew painfully. At least he was in good company with the likes of Steve Jobs; maybe he could get a job at Apple after this was all over?

He picked up his phone, hoping to chat with someone from his team to talk them out of their decision. He tried everyone on the board one number at a time. No one picked up.

Andrew was even more upset. It didn't look like he could talk his way out of this one. He loved his company, but one too many rash decisions had done him in. His immediate wants had trumped his own long-term gain.

He dialed Chloe, his confidante, his best-friend. She answered, and he immediately felt better. He gave her the full run down and read the letter to her.

"I didn't know the house would cost so much," Chloe said regretfully, choking back her own tears.

"I should have known about the investments Chlo'. It's my fault." Andrew said.

In truth, Andrew had no idea the board would be so heavy handed, but ignorance is never a good excuse. He should have known this might happen.

Andrew continued, "We still have the house Chlo', we just need to figure out our next steps. I know we can make something work."

"Come home, hunny, I'll make us a nice dinner and we can have a nice long talk," Chloe said.

"I'll be right there. Thanks for being amazing, as always," Andrew said.

They then exchanged goodbyes and I love yous and Andrew headed home.

Andrew knew they'd get through this new curveball. They'd learn from it, and things would be okay in the end.

- -

As millennial entrepreneurs, we are faced with the desire to get what we want right now. Let's face it, there isn't much stopping us. For the most part, if we want something bad enough, we can get it. There is a very low barrier to entry if we want a new fancy car, a show dog, or freedom from a corporate job. There are eventual consequences for each decision (debt from buying a car, taking care of a dog, and financial instability), but none of these examples present immediate problems.

There is a term in Freudian psychoanalysis called *the pleasure principle* which is the instinctual seeking out of pleasure and the avoidance of pain. It's how we operate from the core of survival, and what guides the *id* (another Freudian term). The pleasure principle guides our most basic decisions and is strongest when we are younger and the only thought in our heads is "food!"

The superego, on the other hand, is our moral backbone and the cricket on our shoulder imploring us to "always let our conscience be our guide." It's what shows us how much we have to gain by saving money, sticking with a failing business for a potential upswing, and enduring the hard times of a marriage to come out stronger on the other end.

These two opposing forces are interceded upon by the *ego* and are what we need to master.

If we don't find a balance point between the part of ourselves that says, "Give it to me now!" and the part that says, "You know what, self? Go ahead and skip out on this for now," we will lose to our *id* and not find happiness. The power will shift in favor of the *superego* and we may not find what we are looking for.

There is a point in which it makes sense to cash out. Infinite delays of gratification can be debilitating. Reaping the rewards of hard labor is part of the motivation to do the hard work in the first place. Timing becomes key, and so does listening to both our *id* and our *superego* to choose which path makes the most sense.

So how do we do this? How do we know the right time to cash out or to take that risk, or to say no to what seems like a really good opportunity? How do we find that delicate balance between the rush of sweet satisfaction now, vs. the *pièce de résistance* of years of hard work turned luxurious retirement?

It's not easy, and mastery comes with time, but we start by growing up a little bit, choosing what matters in our lives, and designating our top priorities.

Once we know what truly matters and what will move us toward our goals, we will be that much more inclined to avoid the side roads and the easy wins to find long-term success. As unstoppable entrepreneurs, neither will we be so blinded by what could be that we avoid letting loose every once in a while and enjoying the present moment.

Our ultimate happiness doesn't lie in setting bigger and better goals, nor does it rest on how much money we have to show for it during retirement; happiness lies in enjoying the present while planning for the future.

We might have ten good years left. We might have twenty. We also might have three days ticking on an unseen clock. We don't know. Some folks get so caught up in this mindset they seek to live every day to the fullest and are unable to reap the rewards of growth over time. Other folks plan plan plan and don't enjoy most of their time on this Earth. The former doesn't have a future to live for, and the latter ends up living a boring and unfulfilled life.

The mindset of a winning entrepreneur is this: I will live like I only have today and I will plan like I have the rest of my life.

This means enjoying and appreciating every moment, but also working towards delayed gratification and unprecedented enjoyment later on. Ask yourself what your legacy will be and how you will impact others.

What are you giving back that will extend beyond your own life and create good for years to come?

The mark of a life well lived is having no regrets, and this includes living each day and crushing each year. Entrepreneurs grasp this fact better than most, but I believe we struggle with being too extreme. There are some days we are ready to throw in the towel and call it quits, and other days we could see ourselves in it for years. Sometimes we are just a hot mess.

Let's break it down and find some balance.

I Will Live Like I Only Have Today

What are your first thoughts when you hear this statement? What would it mean for you to live like you only have today?

Maybe for you it's spending time with those closest to you, spending one last night on the town, or driving across the US to see California or Maine for the first time.

There aren't many scenarios in which we have advanced notice of our sudden impending death as the clock strikes midnight. There are real-life instances in which weeks or months to live could be something you're faced with, but if we have only one day we probably won't know it.

This is what makes finding balance so hard!

My wife and I have talked often about being smart and not irresponsible when it comes to living life to the fullest. We still have student loans and pay rent. But we often wonder how to live in the present moment and enjoy today, while also building a better future. Were we crazy to go to Thailand for two months rather than put that money towards savings or paying off debt? Maybe. But we want to err on the side of enjoying life and finding richness in experiences, rather than "just being okay."

No one wants to live an "okay" life. I know you don't. The million-dollar question then is how do you appreciate now without jeopardizing the future? If you wait until you have "enough" it could be too late.

My modus operandi is to wait until it makes sense. This is changing with recent events. We are living in a way that errs on the side of going beyond our comfort zone and seeing more of the world. The personal growth and confidence we've gained from travelling and seeing new places has been life-changing, but of course it has its challenges.

The key is to mix in as much real-world planning as you can in order to offset the inherent risk of living in the moment. If you want to take an adventure, plan it for three months down the line, and then get on the ball to make it happen. There's no guarantee you'll be around for another three months, but the risk of missing out on the adventure goes way up if you plan it for five years out and then never take any steps to make it happen.

We all know people who say "I'll travel someday." "Someday" usually means "never."

Don't wait around to enjoy the world and grasp at all it has to offer. Go and make new memories. Make plans to get every delicious bite you can out of this beautiful life. Make the most out of every day and seek to become the best version of you.

I Will Plan Like I Have the Rest of My Life

In the US, Life expectancy is 81.2 years for females and 76.4 years for males. If you are getting close to those ages, live now before it's too late. For everyone else, you most likely have a few more years left. If you are reading this, it's not too late.

Morbid conversations are uncomfortable, but it's important to think about these things. Remembering our mortality helps us to make realistic plans and to hunker down and hustle when we need to so that we can do bigger and even crazier things later on in life.

As a healthy and reasonably fit thirty-year-old male, I can plan for another 46.4 years. This means I haven't even crossed the middle ground of my life. This gives me a sense that I can spend more time in the planning, hustling, and working stages and not have to worry that I am missing out on having fun. But we never know!

Making sure to have a solid set of life goals, clear priorities, and the gumption to say no to fun things now to say yes to even better things later, becomes the lens through which we make important life decisions. Stop believing FOMO (fear of missing out) exists and be okay with spending your Friday nights and weekends brainstorming and putting the axe to the grindstone. I've done it, and while it isn't fun to miss out on game nights, the latest designer clothes, or a beach trip with close friends, it's worth the payoff of being able to travel, write books, and live the life that I want to live.

Build a life in which you get to say yes when you want to most. Do you want to spend your hard-earned money on fancy dinners and weekly massages? Great, but maybe that means you can't afford to go skiing in the alps next Christmas. Balance.

The choice is yours in what to make of this one life. There is no one else directing your path and no one else can decide what it is you truly want.

If you want to live like a champion later on, put in the hard work now and don't be worried that you're losing your ability to have fun. There will be time for that. Keep pushing and eventually you will get yours.

Strive for a balance to discover your true potential. Work the yin and the yang to live a life overflowing with joy, happiness, and contentment.

INSTANT WIN VS. DELAYED GRATIFICATION SELF-RATING

Do you constantly seek easy and instantaneous wins? Or do you focus solely on future goals and big wins later on? Mark the spot where you tend to lean or check the box if you have balance in this area. We will revisit these later on so you can build your personal balance blueprint.

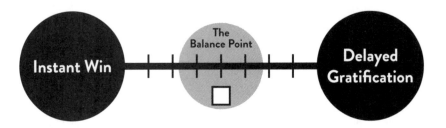

CHAPTER NINE

HUSTLE VS. HEALTH

*"Things may come to those who wait, but only
the things left by those who hustle."*
—Abraham Lincoln

"You're only one workout away from a good mood."
—Unknown

Andrew laced up his running shoes and went for a run for the first time in two months.

The house on the lake was amazing, but it was taking every bit of his time and effort to afford to keep it. He had even enlisted Chloe to help with time-intensive tasks like data collection, emails, and product listings whenever she wasn't taking care of baby Lily.

It almost wasn't enough. He was burning the midnight oil every night and waking up at the crack of dawn every morning to stay ahead. He had built a new online business selling specialized wood carvings, but the remaining money from his investment withdrawal was running out, and he needed to turn a profit soon.

He looked down at his ample gut and shook his head in disgust. He picked up the pace, determined to make this run count.

It was horrible and refreshing and by the end his dogs were barking, but the run was exactly what he needed. He was glad to sweat for a second. He could feel the stress of being overworked washing away.

When he got back, Chloe met him at the door with a smile on her face. "Well hey there, good lookin!"

"Hey to yourself," Andrew said with a wink.

Chloe opened the door for Andrew and said, suddenly very serious, "Hunny, I'm so proud of you for going on a run. You are always motivating me to do just a little bit more. Thanks for being incredible."

Andrew smiled at his wife and said, "Of course my dear! I'm sorry that I go into these phases and let myself go. I am just doing what I can for the family..." As he said this Andrew's smile vanished and his head sagged.

Chloe gave Andrew a hug. "You could do nothing for the rest of your life and I'd still love you, you know that right? But you gotta stop and think every once in a while eh? We need you around long-term."

"Thanks my love," whispered Andrew. "I'll focus more on my own health, that's a promise. And by the way, it's shower time. Wanna join?"

"I'm doing the shopping this morning," Chloe said, smiling.

"I'll take care of it later today," suggested Andrew.

Still smiling, Chloe said nothing and started walking back upstairs. As she reached the top she turned around, made a slight "come here" motion with her hand, and kept walking.

"What a day!" Andrew thought as he giddily sauntered up the steps. He'd have to work out more often!

- -

Hustling and healthy living are two competing entities destined to be at odds with each other for all eternity. It's a battle between the two forces, and if you aren't careful, you could get sucked so far to one side that you're either A) a chunky nerd with his face buried in a laptop every hour of the day or B) A fit but broke couch surfer who spends all his/her time rock climbing.

We don't need to live as unhealthy entrepreneurs, nor do we need to give up on the hustle in order to be healthy. We can be vibrant, healthy, and fit all while maintaining a dedicated work ethic. Don't be a chunky nerd or a fit couch surfer. Learn to find a balance between the two forces and live a long and healthy life.

Over the past two years of being a full-time entrepreneur I've had to be viciously intentional with taking breaks, spending time with people, and exercising. For the most part, I don't struggle with getting into the hustler's mindset, and most entrepreneurs don't once they get the train going. But neither do I spend all of my time working. I've hit on a delicate balance in this area, and I want to share how it can be a reality for you too. Hustlers can be healthy if they strive to be intentional and adhere to positive daily habits.

How to Not be a Chunky Nerd

I purposefully make sure to do something active every single day. I have to. I spend most of the day at a computer staring at a screen. If you are one of the many entrepreneurs who spends most of their day huddled in the corner of a coffee shop you'll find this section useful.

It's not easy to be consistently motivated to do something active. Some days it's going to rain, you're not going to feel like driving to the gym, or you're going to have a pile of work calling out to you.

Fight the pull to be lazy. Do something physically active every day. It's basic advice, and in practice it works, but it's challenging to implement. Condition your body to do at least one active thing each day for thirty minutes. Take a walk, go on quick run, or do yoga from your living room.

Beyond doing one thing every day, here are some other helpful tips for entrepreneurs to avoid chunky nerd syndrome:

1) Get a Standing Desk.

I bought one for around $300 and it has become my favorite piece of furniture. It goes up when I want to stand. It goes down when I want to sit. Easy peasy. I end up standing most of the day, which has its own problems, but it's better than sitting the whole time for sure.

You can also get a product like a *Nexstand* which works as a portable laptop stand. It helps correct my posture when sitting down working, and also prompts me to stand if the coffee shop or coworking space has taller desks for working. It's a great way to avoid back problems and the feeling of being hunched over a laptop for hours.

Key tip: For best results sitting or standing, line up the middle of your screen with your line of sight for the optimal ergonomic setup. Also, mix periods of sitting with standing to avoid overdoing it, especially at first.

2) Eat Better Foods

We are what we eat. The food that we put in our bodies matters. My wife and I did the Whole30 recently and I can tell you that eating mostly veggies for thirty straight days gives you more real energy than pounding coffees.

Ask yourself why you are putting certain foods into your body. Sure, sometimes we need to get a quick zap of energy to finish a big project, but most other times we would be better served by eating a healthy salad or a home-cooked healthy meal.

3) Don't Neglect Sleep!

Sleep is the very first activity that gets the axe when we hustle. Why? Because we don't prioritize it, and we think we can replace sleep with coffee, green tea, or sugary drinks. This works in the short term, but sleep deprivation is no joke. Our long-term success and fulfillment in life will not be realized if we only sleep for a few hours each night.

Crushing it with the hustle means deprioritizing other wants and needs for short periods of time, but don't get locked into the idea that the only way to truly hustle is to lose sleep.

Sleep is the body's best line of defense against sickness and is the only natural way to recover lost energy. Not prioritizing sleep is a mistake. Utilize your prime hours when working, and be sure to average at least eight hours every night. Be in it for the long haul.

4) Take Breaks Often.

Consider the use of the pomodoro technique[17] for time management and remembering to take breaks. Developed by Francesco Cirillo in the late 1980s, this technique works like this:

1) Pick your task to be completed.

2) Set the pomodoro timer to 25 minutes and begin working.

3) When the timer goes off, put a checkmark down on a piece of paper (or find an app that will keep track for you).

4) Take a short five-minute break and start the timer again.

5) Once you repeat this and have four checkmarks, take a longer break of fifteen to thirty minutes.

---

17 "The Pomodoro Technique® - Proudly Developed by Francesco Cirillo | Cirillo Consulting GmbH." Cirillo Company. Accessed June 08, 2019. https://francescocirillo.com/pages/pomodoro-technique.

This method of time management is just one of many tricks you can use to remember to take breaks. Your overall productivity will increase if you find a method like this to keep your head in the game. The time you spend working will be more productive.

Don't do more than a few hours of hardcore focused work without taking a break. Dance around the house, take a walk to check the mail, or call your mom. Step away from the hustle and do something else other than stare at your computer screen.

5) Join a Nearby Gym.

Give yourself the option of working out at any time of day, no matter what the weather looks like. Stuck with writer's block or sick of emails? Go to the gym and get a workout in.

If you have a Planet Fitness around you, for ten bucks a month you can have 24/7 fitness available at your fingertips. Give it a try and it might help to keep your fitness levels up. Also consider taking a book along to read instead of getting in more screen time.

6) Take Advantage of Nice Weather

If the weather is nice, plan a long walk, go for a run, or take advantage of outdoor bootcamp workouts. The fresh air is good for you and will do your entire body a service.

Take it one step further and go on a hike. Studies show time in nature can reduce obsessive or negative thoughts[18] and can even improve

---

18   Bratman, Gregory N., J. Paul Hamilton, Kevin S. Hahn, Gretchen C. Daily, and James J. Gross. "Nature Experience Reduces Rumination and Subgenual Prefrontal Cortex Activation." PNAS. July 14, 2015. Accessed June 08, 2019. https://www.pnas.org/content/112/28/8567.

creative problem solving.[19] Do your body and mind a favor and spend time disconnected from our increasingly connected world.

7) Reduce Stress

Too much stress is not good for our bodies. Fight stress with deep breathing techniques and take extra breaks if you find yourself stressed out by email, a frustrating client, or an employee who isn't working out.

Don't let your work and the hustle stop you from enjoying life and having fun. Stress is not something we need to accept as part of the gig. At times it's unavoidable, but be sure to take positive action steps to reduce your stress.

8) Seek to Become Anti-Fragile

The first time I ever heard the term anti-fragile was in a book called *Level Up Your Life* by Steve Kamb.[20] In the book, Kamb discusses the idea to make our bodies more resistant to the world. As an entrepreneur and health and fitness coach, Kamb believes in the value of making our bodies strong so we can do the things we like to do.

The idea of anti-fragility is a unique perspective on health. No longer are you working out just because you feel like you should, but to experience more in life. If you want to travel more and do more, you will be much more apt and able if you are anti-fragile.

This means you can take a skiing vacation, hike the Appalachian

19   Atchley, Ruth Ann, David L. Strayer, and Paul Atchley. "Creativity in the Wild: Improving Creative Reasoning through Immersion in Natural Settings." PLOS ONE. Accessed June 08, 2019. https://journals.plos.org/plosone/article ?id=10.1371/journal.pone.0051474.

20   Kamb, Steve. *Level up Your Life: How to Unlock Adventure and Happiness by Becoming the Hero of Your Own Story*. New York, NY: Rodale, 2016.

Mountains, or even run a marathon in Italy. Don't stymie your future experiences with the limitations you've placed on yourself by not prioritizing health and fitness. Don't be a chunky nerd who can't walk up two flights of stairs without getting winded. Life is rich with potential experiences and joy. Make yourself anti-fragile so you can experience everything life has to offer.

How to Not be a Fit but Broke Couch Surfer

The hustle is not all bad. In fact, sometimes hustling is the only true way to get something worthwhile accomplished in a short amount of time. I wrote my last book, *Volcanic Momentum*, in three weeks' time. I couldn't have done it without some serious hustle.

Hustle means working it to the nth degree. It means staying up late hours. It means completing the deliverable at whatever cost, even if that cost is sleep, exercise, and potentially, your closest relationships.

Author and extremely successful entrepreneur Gary Vaynerchuck (Gary Vee) is probably the most well-known proponent of the power of the hustle. In his book *Crush It,*[21] he shares that it takes late nights "bleeding from the eyeballs" staying up until 2 AM to find success. Then waking up at 5 AM to start all over.

I don't disagree with Gary here, and I think his advice is spot on for someone who has an itch to get started. The problem is that this pace is not sustainable. No one can live off of three hours of sleep and continue to function well for the long term. And since the long term is what we are after, we have to be extremely careful about how we use the hustle to our advantage.

---

21   Vaynerchuk, Gary. *Crush It!: Why NOW Is the Time to Cash in on Your Passion.* New York: Harper Business, an Imprint of HarperCollins Publishers, 2017.

But, if we are careful, the hustle is a powerful tool in the entrepreneur's arsenal. We can learn to use it when it's needed and tuck it away when it's not. Our health won't suffer major effects on account of working late or getting up really early every once in a while.

I'd like to share several key points to utilize the hustle to finish tasks, get things done, and crush it:

- Don't forget to drink water. Probably a duh, but it's a good reminder anyway. When's the last time you had a sip of the liquid that makes up most of our DNA? Take a break from reading and go get some.

- Have a big project you need to finish? Take a night or two a week to stay up late and put in the hours. Get up early and work on the project before anything else.

- Be willing to put the time in when it's needed. Don't think that just because you work for yourself, you shouldn't work past five every day. Most likely you'll need to work past five and even past midnight to get your business rolling.

- Organize your day and be intentional. This will save you from having to hustle every day to meet your goals. The more organized and disciplined you are, the more valuable the time you spend becomes. Plan to get the work done and it will get done.

- Focus up. When you go into the hustle mode, focus on your biggest goal. If you end up distracted by Instagram, YouTube, or emails, the hustle will turn into a six-hour work session that didn't really move the needle forward on your important items.

- Fail quickly, move on, and try again. Don't let a setback set you back. Embrace failure and use it as a stepping stone to finding success.

- Check your motivation and keep dreaming. What is the hard work for? Who is going to benefit from your hard work? Is there a good chance it's going to lead to a big result? You might not know the answers and that's okay; but it's easier to hustle if you have a solid driving point. Imagining what could be is a one of the entrepreneur's greatest tools to keep on pushing. When the hustle gets monotonous and you're exhausted, sometimes you just need to take a second to check the bigger picture.

- Say no to fun things. In order to hustle you have to find the time. Friday night might be the best night to hustle. Instead of relaxing and taking a breather on Sunday afternoons and evenings, I write. What is one thing you could give up and hustle instead?

If you struggle to get into the hustle and would rather do good things for your body like sleep, run, or make a healthy meal, remember that we can't have it all. It's okay to go to Starbucks after 8 PM, grab a cup of joe and a brownie, and get to work, as long as it doesn't become an everyday habit.

Most entrepreneurs know this intrinsically, but here's another reminder not to feel shame over missing out on hanging with friends or skipping dinner to fix a problem for a client. It's going to happen.

Hustle when needed, and be quick to jump back to the healthy side when the hustle becomes like a new love. Don't marry the hustle! Step back, breathe the fresh air, grab a healthy snack, and only hit it hard when you need to.

If you can master this one area of being a balanced entrepreneur, you will find success. Learning when to push and when to stop is how you keep going. To be in it for the long haul and truly find success, learn to hustle when needed, and establish healthy habits you can quickly return to when the hustle is over.

Do this and your journey to balance is almost complete.

HUSTLE VS. HEALTH SELF-RATING

Do you hustle into the midnight hours or do you put your health above all else? Mark or circle the spot where you tend to lean or check the box if you have balance in this area. We will revisit these later on so you can build your personal balance blueprint.

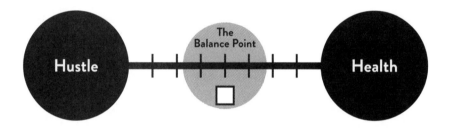

CHAPTER TEN

THE 80% VS. 20%

"The greatest heroes are those who do their duty in the daily grind of domestic affairs whilst the world whirls as a maddening dreidel."
—Florence Nightingale

"We were not sent into this world to do anything into which we cannot put our hearts."
—Andrew Ruskin

With a loud "thwack!" the computer mouse shattered into a hundred tiny pieces, bouncing off the wall and raining down on the office floor in a shower of flying debris.

With a guttural "argh" Andrew stepped out his office and dove onto the floor of his bedroom in anguish.

Peering out of the bathroom in fear, Chloe first walked into the office. Upon seeing the shards of what was once a perfectly good computer mouse littering the floor, her suspicions of what had occurred were confirmed.

"Come here my love," She said as she walked into the bedroom. "I got you."

She sat down on the ground next to a sobbing Andrew. Not used to seeing him like this she was unsure what to do, but she sat quietly next to him.

"I can't do this anymore," Andrew said.

"You can't do what?"

"I'm tapped out. I can't be the person I should be. I can't do this. I can't…"

"Andrew, stop it. You know you are more than good enough for me. Good enough for your family. Good enough for yourself," Chloe responded.

"I want it all Chlo'. The second I think I have an idea of what I should do and I try it, something else gets in the way. Something always suffers. Someone gets hurt because I'm not good enough."

"Andrew Lincoln Wells. I don't want to hear any more of it. So what if you failed with your business ideas? So what if it took years to figure out I was the number-one person in your life? So what that you've made terrible decisions along the way?"

You're not filling me with a lot of confidence, love," Andrew quickly interjected.

"I'm not done," Chloe said with a determined nod. "So what if most of your first instincts turn out poorly? Look at all we have now and all that we've accomplished together. Look at our beautiful daughter."

As she said this Lily bounded into the room with the biggest smile on her face. She had been playing dress up in her closet and hadn't heard the commotion.

"Why are you on the floor mommy. You're a silly bucket," Lily said, laughing. She came bounding in for a hug wearing long rainbow socks, a Halloween bear mask, and an Iron Man tee shirt.

"I don't deserve you Chlo'," Andrew said with a whisper into Chloe's ear as the family sat there, hugging tightly. "Also, we have a pretty strange child."

Chloe whispered back, "No, you don't, but you're stuck with me and I with you, my dear. And oh yes, we do indeed."

Andrew looked over at Lily and said, "Isn't that right, angel? You're one little weirdo huh? What are you wearing today, munchkin?"

Lily smiled and said, "I wanted to look like Daddy today."

Andrew sat there in stunned silence while Chloe roiled with laughter. Soon everyone joined in and in that moment, Andrew was content.

- -

What is the 80% of work taking up most of your time this week?

What is the 20% you are working on today?

What are the most important tasks we need to complete this week even if all else fails?

Such questions are often thrown around the Ring household. Yes, we are odd ducks! But we have seen the power of the 80/20 principle firsthand.

We've also seen the power of overwhelm, and how the 80% whirlwind can be so consuming that it leaves you feeling empty and not good enough. It can sap out every last bit of strength from your body, mind and soul. Mastering how to tackle the 80% is something to get right.

The 80/20 rule, or the "Pareto Principle," first coined by the Italian economist Vilfredo Pareto, way back in 1895,[22] says that 20% of

---

22   Pareto, Vilfredo, Aldo Montesano, Alberto Zanni, and Luigino Bruni. *Manual of Political Economy: A Variorum Translation and Critical Edition.* Oxford: Oxford University Press, 2013.

people are divided into the "vital few" of society and the other 80% into the "trivial many."

It works the same way in churches and other organizations. 20% of the members end up doing 80% of the work.

Pareto purported that this very same principle carries over and applies directly to life and business. If you were to make a list of ten items on a to-do list, two of the items will bring about 80% of the results. The other eight items will only bring about 20% of the results.

Move this into a time-management/productivity realm and you'll see 80% of our results come from 20% of our efforts. Focus is key.

The battle rages between the 80% and 20%, in life and in business!

For our purposes we will break down the 80% and 20% like this: The 20% is what you need to do to move the needle forward and push towards lifelong goals, and the 80% is the work you need to do to keep the lights on and the bills paid.

Each avenue is important and takes time, but the 80% is the gold-plated dragon of busyness that threatens to eat you. If you get eaten by the 80% dragon, you can't work on what's important. So sad, but at least you were a tasty snack.

Don't get eaten. Use the 80/20 principle to master your time and establish a set of priorities in your daily life.

Consider the importance of tackling the 80% and crushing that work, but leaving just enough time and energy to work on the important stuff. Let's face it friend, if you spend your time chasing your tail without a solid long-term goal and a way out, then what are you doing?

We need not stay stuck forever in whatever issue we face. We are never stuck. Maybe it's underpaying work, clients we don't love, or maybe we have other interests that we'd rather devote time to. There is always a way out of work we don't love.

Even if you love what you do, there exists a 20% task that will help you maintain the work you are doing. The 20% will give you the energy you need to get through the daily grind, knowing that you have a future-oriented task giving you long-term potential.

We are either moving forward or falling backwards; the 80% exists to keep us moving forward, while the 20% work is our path to the next level.

Not Getting Smacked Down by the 80%

The 80% is important. What you do with most of your time each day is of paramount importance to your success.

I was confused by this when I was a level-one entrepreneur. I knew I wanted to grow, so I spent most of my time working towards big future goals and eventually got sucked in. My everyday life suffered for the massive amount of attention I spent on working toward these goals. I wasn't putting enough time and attention on my job, self-care, or my relationships.

I'm grateful Miranda planned fun events on the weekends with friends or else I would have spent those weekends alone in a coffee shop, typing away on my keyboard. I was acting as if normal life could be paused while I pursued my dreams.

Everyone has their 80%. It could be a busy job, raising a family, community responsibilities, health problems, or any number of things that demand your attention. You might be at a place where life isn't as busy and you have very few responsibilities outside yourself; even still, we all have to contend with some sort of "busyness" in our everyday lives. How we approach this makes all the difference in our journey to success.

The most challenging part of finding balance here is the mindset behind the whirlwind of life's everyday struggles and responsibilities. The 80% is this whirlwind we cannot ignore, but if we pay it too much heed it sucks us up. Often it involves tasks that we don't like doing or that feel painful to complete in a timely manner. It's important to stick with it, and know that once you finish, you can move on to bigger and better things.

I'll be honest here. I struggle with the 80% and the daily grind of life's tasks. As an INFJ with a top-level CliftonStrengths test of "Futuristic" I am quite content with working towards my goals. In fact, I am grateful for the way I see the world as it makes me especially adept at working towards long-term goals.

The problem? Dealing with the here-and-now, forming positive habits, and getting done what needs to get done regardless of my feelings towards it. This is painstakingly challenging. I constantly struggle with doing what I need to do now in order to be able to do what I want later on.

The 80% kicks my butt. Each moment I spend taking out the trash, doing taxes, or getting the car an oil change is time wasted. I don't have time for these tasks. I do them, but I don't like it.

This has uniquely positioned me to be able to write and provide insight into the struggle you have either faced or will face. Can you relate? Do you have such great passion and focus for what you deem to be the most important life tasks, but struggle with the day-to-day?

Take caution that the 20% doesn't become all-consuming and detrimental to your current situation and real-life needs.

Here are some ways to stay focused on the 80% even when you'd rather be doing anything else:

- Remember that each life stage and trial has a story you can share with the world. Focus on the here-and-now to get done what you need to get done.

- Set aside specific times and days in which you'll do the 20% (work during your best hours) so that the rest of your time is spent either taking a break or working on keeping the whirlwind at bay.

- Check email once or twice per day. Skip checking email on weekends. Respond in a timely manner and don't feel bad if it sometimes takes a few days to get back to someone. Some industries won't allow for a multiple-day email response time, but if you can follow this, your busy life will become much easier.

- Be social. As an introvert AND someone who is future-focused AND an online entrepreneur I have to focus on being social. If I'm not intentional about spending time out of my Batcave I'd never see anybody. People give us energy and help us grow. Don't neglect relationships, as they are critical to surviving in this crazy world.

- Boost your productivity. Get more done in less time by reading productivity books or taking courses. Our most valuable asset, time, can be utilized to a greater extent than we know. Spend time thinking about and learning how to do what you do more efficiently with the same level of success.

- Know that your current circumstances will change, whether for good or bad. When I found myself at a day job vacuuming for hours, working as the dishwasher when he didn't show up, or giving a tour while simultaneously trying to answer the phone, I'd be stressed and frustrated. I was spending time NOT doing what I wanted to do most. But circumstances change. Eventually, you'll find yourself spending more and more of your time doing what you love the most. Just remember it probably won't happen overnight. Take the hits as they come and work toward your dream.

- Get help: Hire help in the form of VAs or other employees to take the burden off of you and free up time for important tasks. Be willing to let go and build your business around good people. Learn to delegate and build a team around you to let you do what you do best.

Master Your 20%

In order to master the 20% and spend time reaching towards your biggest life goals, consider getting into the habit of doing this work first.

Brian Tracy, a world-renowned self-help expert, recommends "Eating the Frog First."[23] He shares that doing the most important task first helps us to move the needle forward while also giving us daily momentum to have a productive workday. This is particularly helpful when learning to give the 20% the attention it deserves.

---

23 Tracy, Brian. "The 80 20 Rule Explained (a.k.a. Pareto Principle) | Brian Tracy." Brian Tracy's Self Improvement & Professional Development Blog. November 28, 2018. Accessed June 08, 2019. https://www.briantracy.com/bl og/personal-success/how-to-use-the-80-20-rule-pareto-principle/.

The 20% involves tasks which move your long-term goals forward, yet can be hard to find time and energy to accomplish. These goals and tasks include:

- Reading the latest book about your number-one passion.
- Journaling every day.
- Choosing to eat a healthy dinner and get a good workout.
- Spending time brainstorming what your purpose in life is (or at least your direction).
- Blocking out time every day for non-urgent tasks.

If you find yourself sucked up by the whirlwind of life, and unable to work towards your higher purpose and destiny, build margins into your life so you can grow in this area. Get up earlier, say no to TV, or sell the boat to free up Sunday afternoons. Everyone can create margins in their lives, however small, to focus on what's truly important. We are never too busy for our top priorities.

I've been a long-time advocate of *The Four Disciplines of Execution*[24] as outlined in the book of the same name in which Chris McChesney, Sean Covey and Jim Huling talk about the whirlwind of work and how we keep it at bay by doing the most demanding tasks first. They share that what we miss is the push to do the deeper, more meaningful work that will actually move our goals forward. The whirlwind will bring us crashing down unless we focus on the wildly important.

"Avoiding the danger of the whirlwind" and "doing the important work first" are two more phrases tossed around regularly in the Ring household. My wife and I are convinced that the needle of our

---

24   McChesney, Chris, Sean Covey, and Jim Huling. *The 4 Disciplines of Execution: Achieving Your Wildly Important Goals.* New York: Free Press, 2016.

Destiny Goals (our most important and impactful life goals) won't move forward unless we focus on the important tasks first.

It's hard to focus on the wildly important; being successful with an 80/20 strategy involves an intentionality with your time. It starts with having weekly meetings with an accountability partner, a close-knit group of friends or business partners, or even a regular Skype call with your entrepreneur friend who lives in Bali.

Your 2o% is going to be unique to you and your situation. Right now, my 20% is writing, blogging, and spending time marketing my own books. I know I want to eventually be a full-time author, but for now I spend roughly 20% of my time working towards this goal. Eventually, the wildly important will become my main point of focus, and this is where the magic happens. As I build toward this future, I can spend more of my time on what I deem to be the most important, while not ignoring real-world responsibilities.

Figure out what you want your 20% to be and go for it! Your 20% will change over time (mine surely has!), so don't wait for the perfect next step in order to take the more important first step.

Ask yourself:

1) Do I know what my wildly important tasks are as they relate to my goals?

2) If not, what can I do to find out? (Read, ask a friend, brainstorm).

3) If yes, am I consistently following through and completing my weekly goals?

4) Do I have an accountability partner to help keep track of my progress?

5) What is keeping me from spending time in the realm of the

20%? What life busyness is keeping me from doing what I know I need to do?

Even though I've known the power of the above for years, I still fall into the trap of busyness. Avoiding the pressures and demands of life might seem impossible, but I've developed a few strategies for conquering those issues and getting done what I need to get done:

- The most important step here is knowing what your 20% is. What do you want to accomplish in life? Where do you see yourself in five years? What are you most passionate about right now? Such questions should bring clarity to your 20% tasks.

- Do your best work at your best time of day. Some gurus say to do your most important work in the morning. This is bad advice if you don't do well in the mornings. I'm not a morning guy and I know at least a few of you reading this will relate. Pick the time of day that you are most "with it" and do your 20% tasks then.

- Pick a day and avoid as much of the 80% as you can. Don't forget to pick up the kids from school or eat breakfast, but if you can take a day to focus up and get important work done, then do it.

- As you go through your week, take note of the tasks you'd love to get done. Don't feel pressured to do them right away, but having a special 20% to-do list can be helpful when you get to work.

- Know there will be days and potentially even weeks at a time that get bogged down with life. Things happen. People get sick. Life gets hard. Pick yourself up when the dust clears and get back to it.

Once you start to find time for the 2o%, a curious thing usually happens. More and more time is put toward these activities and the 80% starts to suffer. Such is life. The delicate balance an entrepreneur strikes is crucial for long-term health and wellbeing. Thus we have to tackle both areas.

Use this 80/20 metric as a guideline. You might choose to spend more time on the wildly important 20%, but don't neglect the 80%. Focus each day on the important goals, put out any big fires that occur, and build a future you will be happy living in. Over time you'll find success, and you'll craft a perfect work/life balance.

The 80% is what everyone else who isn't an entrepreneur is doing better than you. To them, it's all there is. All they need to do is focus on getting through the day, doing well at their job, and getting by. You know who I'm talking about, and this person isn't you.

You know the importance of working on long-term goals and of getting out of the rat race to pursue your own endeavors, goals, and the wildest longings of your heart.

Be wary of the pull away from what needs to get done; spend an appropriate amount of time working on your most important items; and never forget to pivot along the way if needed. Do this, and you will be one hell of a successful entrepreneur.

80% VS. 20% SELF-RATING

Do you spend all of your time in the whirlwind of life's busy-ness or doing only what you know you were born to do? Mark the spot where you tend to lean or check the box if you have balance in this area. We will revisit these at the end of the book so you can build your personal balance blueprint.

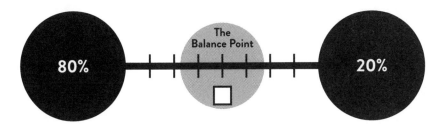

CHAPTER ELEVEN
POTENTIAL VS. CONTENTMENT

*"One way to keep momentum going is to
have constantly greater goals."*
—Michael Korda

*"When you do things from your soul, you
feel a river moving in you, a joy."*
—Rumi

Andrew's journey is over. Now it's your turn. And you have one more decision to make. The battle between working towards our potential and being content with what we have right now reigns in the entrepreneurial life today.

Which will you choose?

Will you be on constant lookout for your next big win and miss the forest for the trees? Will you be so content with your current status that you miss out on your potential?

Again, neither choice is good and right. Neither option is going to lead to success and fulfillment. A balance needs to be struck.

We can have a deeper joy and sense of absolute happiness if we find the balance point. I've saved this battle for last for a reason. If you get nothing else from this book, know this: As an entrepreneur you must learn to be at peace with what could be and what is. If you don't, you'll quickly burn out and crash and burn.

Let me be vulnerable for a second. I've struggled with this throughout my entrepreneurial career. I've had a deep yearning to reach my potential and I'm not content with the small wins that come along. I often find myself shrugging off success and forgetting to celebrate wins along the way. It's not a lack of pride, it's a refusal to be content with what I have. Luckily, my wife makes me celebrate wins and is often more excited than I am, which serves as a reminder of the importance for balance in this realm.

It's obviously important to reach for bigger and better goals, but it can't come at the cost of not appreciating the small but extremely important opportunities we have for contentment.

Learning to be content with what you have now, living a life with no regrets, and also working towards a brighter future is challenging. To do this we need to find joy in the moment and appreciate every second we are on this Earth, while we also work to build a better future. We have no idea if tomorrow could be our very last day, or if we have several decades of fruitful and prosperous years before us. We don't know and thus we have to live as if we are running out of time.

Since you are now a master of planning vs. action and instant win vs. delayed gratification, you'll see the importance of cherishing every moment and realizing that you have more than enough, but also feeling a resolute determination to make the most of your time by reaching your utmost potential.

Mastery in this area is choosing to be happy despite the circum-stances, knowing that where you are right now is exactly where God wants you to be, and still working hard each day to give it your all.

I've battled anxiety and worry all my life, and it's only been over the last few years that I'm learning to experience joy in the moment. Every single day we are here on this Earth is a day we can count ourselves lucky.

So take today and work to appreciate the importance of reaching the highest tier of what you are capable of, but remember to live in the moment and discover true contentment.

Reaching Your Potential

I strongly believe in what the late Jim Rohn, American entrepreneur, author and motivational speaker said about potential:

"The big challenge is to become all that you have the possibility of becoming. You cannot believe what it does to the human spirit to maximize your human potential and stretch yourself to the limit."[25]

Stretching feels oh so good. I stretch every night before I go to bed. It's worth every second and helps me to get to sleep quickly, and I usually wake up feeling refreshed the next day.

We know how good physical stretching is for us, but why do we hesitate to read new books, take the next step for our business, or find a way to work remotely so we can travel the world?

Stretching and having new experiences is how we reach our potential. Trying new ways of doing business won't always work, but at the very least it will refine our current approach. The risk of staying the same and not reaching our potential is too great.

Reaching our potential involves an acute self-awareness and willingness to accept feedback. We have to ask ourselves the hard questions about where we are at right now, like:

- What am I doing with my life?
- Could I be doing more?

---

25 PERSONAL DEVELOPMENT by Jim Rohn. Accessed June 08, 2019. http://guaranteed-success.com/personal-development-by-jim-rohn.

- How can I change my daily actions and habits to work toward self-improvement?
- How am I stretching?
- What am I reaching for?

We can (and should) have bigger and better goals, but if we don't start with ourselves and our skills, our potential is capped early on. As an entrepreneur you know time is your most valuable asset, but deciding what we do with it can be both intoxicating and challenging. You have to first decide that your full potential is something you desire to reach, and then go for it.

Work your business to the next level. Read 100 books this year. Learn a new language or travel to a country where you don't speak the language. Break outside of what you think you are capable of and realize you are destined for more.

When I was growing up, I was happy to trade a full day at the grocery store for a few bucks. As busy entrepreneurs we have to become uber intentional with our time and this means making sure that every day leads us one step closer to our potential.

We become so worried about our time and other assets we are in danger of forgetting the bigger picture. But we can't do this. A balanced life demands that we zoom out and grasp what it is we are doing it all for. Our potential impact on the world hangs in a delicate balance.

Pursue your potential with daily action, a constant re-working of your goals, and a fervent desire to be all that you can be. I don't know you, and yet I know beyond a shadow of a doubt that you have something inside of you the world needs. Go for it and become what you were born to be.

What Potential is Not

Potential is not a list of everything we could possibly do. We will never get to everything, and if we are reaching toward bigger and better goals, some of the items on our lists will be left undone in our lives. Our potential lies within. Our potential means giving the best we can possibly give with the time we have. Reaching for our potential means saying no to everything that doesn't feed our major life goals.

It's also not something we truly ever reach. It's a goal we can't complete. If we did, there'd no longer be any reason to grow. The very nature of reaching for your potential means recognizing that it's a goal we won't reach. It will constantly be just outside of our grasp. The goal, then? To get as we close as we can to maximizing our potential, and enjoying the journey along the way. We must learn balance in this approach and appreciate the moments of growth along the way.

How to be Content in the Moment

Being content means to be in a state of peaceful happiness and joy. It means being okay with what we've accomplished up until this moment. It means being proud of ourselves despite how many items lay unchecked on our to-do lists. Since there will always be more projects we won't ever get to, we must get used to the fact that we will die without finishing our to-do lists. To some of you this is a scary prospect, but it's true. I admit it's hard for me to swallow too since I don't like the idea of being unfinished, but it's a truth we can't escape.

Peace occurs in the moment and isn't tied to external circumstances. You can be out of money, living on the street, and have no job prospects and still be at peace. It's a feeling we can cultivate independent of what might be going on around us. It's like a cancer patient who only has a few months to live and finds joy in living out the rest of their life doing what they always wanted to do but didn't think they could.

Since contentment is a matter of perspective and mindset, the question becomes what can be done about it? How do we experience the emotion of contentment even when everything around us is screaming at us to keep going and keep reaching?

As entrepreneurs it means not getting so lost in what could be with our potential that we miss the moment as it passes. It starts with finding our ultimate passion and purpose. As discussed in an earlier chapter, if we find the balance point between passion and purpose we are better able to find contentment. If our purpose becomes clear and we have an overwhelming passion to see it through, our lives will be richer and more fulfilled than we ever thought possible.

I wanted to share a few easy-to-implement tactics that have worked for me to shift my mindset to find contentment in the moment, even as I am daily reaching towards my potential. Use these tips to find daily contentment:

- Appreciate every moment, especially the moments you spend with the ones you love. Every time I look at my dear Miranda, I am filled with a sense of joy. My heart is most filled when I look upon her sweet face. Who or what brings you the most joy?

- Meditate to find inner joy. There's so much noise in our world. Take a break from input and distraction and take a second to hear yourself think. Pray to your higher power. Think about how others have helped you on your journey. Fill your thoughts with gratitude. Learn to master your inner voice and discover an ability to experience clarity of thought. Bring yourself back to center and the present moment. Doing so has helped me find peace amidst the chaos. I suggest you give it a try, even if it's just fifteen minutes a day.

- Seek out joy and happiness in experiences, not possessions. Experiences turn us into greater people. Acquiring more will only bring happiness for a brief moment and then quickly become a burden, something we have to get rid of.

- Keep a gratitude journal or notebook of all the things you appreciate. This need only take a few minutes per day and can be a great practice for keeping your mind focused on the things that matter most.

- Smile at the next person you see and observe their reaction. It might be all the person needed to get through the day and in just a few seconds you've created a joyful moment for both of you.

Live every day to the fullest by recognizing and appreciating each moment as it passes by.

What Contentment Isn't

Being content doesn't mean you can't be sad or angry or experience other emotions. Do you remember Pixar's *Inside Out?* The entire point of the film was that in order to have the utmost joy, sadness or anger has to be mixed in too. Sometimes the most profound moments of our lives come from the deepest pits of anguish or sorrow which lead to becoming uplifted and joyful in time.

Build a contentment mindset and shift your perspective to embrace the hardships that will come in life, and use your joy muscle to smile a little more brightly than you might have before.

As entrepreneurs, the sooner we can master the art of discovering joy, the happier and more fulfilled our lives will become.

This book is coming to an end, but your next steps are just beginning. Don't leave this book without planning for your next action step today. Seek contentment and live out your best life. Discover contentment, peace, and joy in the moment and continue to reach towards your ultimate potential. Find the line to teeter on and exist there, experiencing the best of both worlds.

POTENTIAL VS. CONTENTMENT SELF-RATING

Are you always reaching toward the next big goal or are you so content with your current circumstances that you might be missing out on your potential to make a difference? Mark the spot where you tend to lean or check the box if you have balance in this area. We will revisit these later on so you can build your personal balance blueprint.

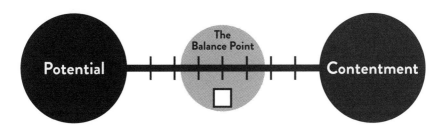

CONCLUSION AND CALL TO TAKE IT UP A NOTCH

Let's take it up a notch, shall we? Let's embrace the true entrepreneur within and finally find balance. Make it your mission to follow the strategies outlined in this book to get moving towards your potential for major success.

From your newly-centered balance point, you can move ahead toward greener pastures flowing with provision, joy, and a sense of fulfillment.

I've presented you with the tools to take stock of your position in several key areas for entrepreneurial balance. Now it's time to get to work, and above all, **don't let the pendulum swing too far.**

Remember the eleven points of contention outlined in this book. For each option, look back into the book to remember which one you resonate with most. If you're right on the balance point, check the box. If not, pay special attention to the strategies in the corresponding section and get to work.

Here are the eleven areas again:
1) Preparation vs. Action
2) Work vs. Play
3) Yes vs. No
4) Purpose vs. Passion
5) Reactive vs. Proactive
6) Intention vs. Perception
7) Consumption vs. Production
8) Instant Win vs. Delayed Gratification
9) Hustle vs. Health
10) 80 vs. 20
11) Potential vs. Contentment

Circle two or three of the areas *you* struggle with most. Now highlight two or three you knock out of the park. Celebrate and continue with your strengths, and do your best to grow in your weaknesses.

Now you have a personal blueprint to find your balance point. You know what you do well and what you need to keep working on. If you know you are struggling in particular areas, devote your attention to swinging the pendulum the other way to find balance.

Final Thoughts

Nobody's perfect, right? We all struggle in certain areas. The key is recognizing and understanding what our struggle points are AND what we are really good at so we can focus on the areas that need work.

Once you know your struggle areas, you'll be ready to achieve balance in your own life.

I'm really good at the hustle vs. health, as I always prioritize getting in a good workout and doing my best to eat well, while giving ample time to the hustle when necessary. My past journeys have taught me that it's important for me to work out regularly, since I spend most of my day staring at a computer screen.

On the other hand, I struggle with work vs. play, as "fun" for me would be working and writing all weekend, which only leads to rapid burnout. I've had to be extremely intentional to put the laptop away and get outside or hang out with people in real life for a few days.

Figure out which areas you need to work on and go for it. Find balance and you will find peace within your grasp.

The story is now yours. I wish you the very best of luck with your goals.

THANK YOU

Thanks for reading *The Balance Point*. I hope you've found a level of enjoyment with Andrew's story, found my anecdotes and tips helpful, and most importantly, have come away with real-world action steps you can take right away.

For more on finding balance for entrepreneurs, travel on over to my blog at JMRing.com. There, I put up regular content related to goal setting, entrepreneurship, and living a life outside of the norm. I'd love for you to stop by and drop me a line.

Until then, all the best to you and may God bless your endeavors and bring you ever closer to your Destiny Goals.

–Jordan

OTHER BOOKS BY JORDAN

Volcanic Momentum: Get Things Done by Setting Destiny Goals, Mastering the Energy Code, and Never Losing Steam (http://www.JMRing.com/volcanic-momentum)

Now What? Getting Unstuck in a Sticky World: How Taking Action is the Key to Unlocking Your Ultimate Potential (https://www.JMRing.com/getting-unstuck)

Book Launch Gladiator: The 4 Phase Approach to Kindle Book Marketing Success in 2018 (https://www.JMRing.com/book-launch-gladiator-free-book)

The Action Diet: 35 Practical Weight Loss Tactics as Chronicled by the Fiber Guardian (https://www.JMRing.com/the-action-diet)

Peace with Sweets: The Healthy & Fresh Way to Manage Sugar Intake and Reduce Sugar Cravings (https://www.JMRing.com/peace-with-sweets)

A QUICK FAVOR?

Before you go, stop and do something for me, friend.

If you made it to the end, I'm sure you found the content within valuable or at the very least entertaining.

Do me a solid and leave a review today by following this link: JMRing .com/ReviewBalanceBook

It only takes a second and it goes a long way.

Thank you for reading, and best of luck to you as you become a more balanced and unstoppable entrepreneur.

ABOUT THE AUTHOR

Jordan Ring might seem like an intergalactic task-ninja, but he's an authorpreneur at heart. As good as he is with words, his primary goal is to help people live a life of less talk and more action. When he isn't busy writing, blogging, or out walking, Jordan is also the book marketing and launch guru for clients over at his second home, Archangel Ink. And that's not all; he's also a freelance copywriter, writing coach, consultant—and anything else he can do to keep the lights on and the coffee comin'.

His hobbies include playing on Trello boards, watching Marvel movies, drinking iced coffee, and hanging out with his amazing wife, Miranda. You can see what all he's up to on his site at www.JMRing.com.